Better

before

Bigger

Rethinking
Business Success

NICK CRAMP

Better Before Bigger
Rethinking Business Success

ISBN 978-1-912300-38-9
eISBN 978-1-912300-39-6

Published in 2021 by SRA Books

A CIP record of this book is available from the British Library.

Printed in the UK

Contents

Foreword

If you are anything like me then you will have read numerous books on business improvement and absorbed multiple theories on how to implement organisational change. The majority of these texts tend to draw on their authors' experience and talk about grandiose projects, which although useful in part, can often be difficult to translate into personal, day-to-day experience.

When I first read *Better before Bigger*, I was struck by the immediacy of what Nick was presenting. The text resonated and focused my mind on how change can be both tangible and have significant impact. The reflective nature of the book set me an entirely different challenge to those I had previously read – not just to understand how someone else has applied and made transformations, but to consider how I could make changes based on my opportunities and concerns. The book made me realise that I was in control, and it was within my ability to drive myself and my colleagues towards an attainable vision.

The ideas and techniques that Nick sets out in this book are simultaneously thought provoking and challenging. They forced me to rethink and be accountable, to build systems that would scale to achieve shared and agreed goals. For the first time in my career, the book allowed me to see the legitimacy of taking time away from daily tasks to consider the greater transformation process required. This focus on 'better' was liberating in several ways, as it allowed me to think through my entire journey from the creation of structures and processes to how these could be adapted to support improvement over the coming months and years.

The exercises at the end of each chapter allowed me to reflect on using change levers to build strategies that could *actually* make things happen. These exercises are not generic, they ask you to make commitments and prompt you to personally address your business. As a result, the conclusions I drew had meaning and purpose.

People say that 'the proof of the pudding is in the eating' and with the content of this book I have found this to be true. I have been able to apply these newly learned philosophies to what I do each day. Two notable results from this learning have been: first, I have had the confidence to take on a fresh initiative in a significantly different area to my past 30 years of experience; second, I have begun working alongside new colleagues to establish a change programme that is focusing first on building better structures.

Better before Bigger recognises leadership as it is, a series of paradoxes to which there are no clear answers. The personal commitments at the end of each chapter helped me understand my real-world paradoxes, and from this I was able to better conceive what a successful response could look like.

Throughout the book it is clear that the text is written from the perspective of first-hand experience. This brings a refreshing tone and relevance to the ideas being shared; these are hard-learned lessons turned into meaningful and pragmatic theory, not the other way round.

James Penny
Chief Technology Officer, SysGroup

Introduction

The purpose of this book

This book has been written to assist business leaders whose ambitions exceed their current organisational capability. The advice I share with you will, if implemented correctly, enable you to scale your business further with improved clarity, instilled confidence and increased curiosity.

The purpose of this book is not only to explain why you may feel currently unfulfilled, but most importantly what you should do to change this and how it can be best achieved. However, what we must start with is the 'why?' question. The 'why' question for me always supersedes the 'what we should do?' and the 'how should we do it?' questions. If we can understand why we are in a certain situation and why we feel like we do, then we can make sure we choose the correct solution. It is about understanding the root causes and not just treating symptoms. If you want a quick fix to your challenges, there are more succinct books offering an instant solution. However, if you want to take the time to understand what determines the challenges you face as the leader of a growing business, then this is the book for you.

I will show you how a paradigm shift in your thinking will result in a wholly different approach to how your business operates. This will reframe your relationship with your business and simultaneously create a more sustainable organisational structure.

I will share with you the unique map I have created to guide you from operating an adolescent stage business, overly dependent on its leader, to transforming this business into an autonomous company that can operate without your day-to-day input. I will be using the term adolescent to refer to a business that has progressed through its early years to a stage where it is profitable and growing but not yet in a consistent and predictable manner. This business aspires to become a mature organisation with clearly defined processes and systems that will attract a loyal customer base. What restricts this business from maturing could be a host of factors.

Too many business leaders (me included) have become trapped by their creation and have made a job for themselves rather than a company. As the business has grown, so have the demands on the job. I can empathise with both how this happens and how difficult it can seem to escape this situation.

My goal here is to make you realise that in order to transform your business there needs to be a personal transformation first. A business is by and large a reflection of its leaders in its values, culture and mindsets. So it makes sense that the initial change required is by the person(s) who has the greatest influence over the business, which in most cases is the leader or the leadership team. *This is about you first and your business second.*

In the famous paraphrase of Mahatma Gandhi, 'Be the change you want to see in the world.'

Does this resonate?

Have a look through the statements below and see if any resonate with you. Do they apply to the way you are currently feeling about yourself and your business?

➤ I thought success would feel different from this.

➤ I want to continue growing my business, but I need to simultaneously remove myself from being the focal point of its operational side.

➤ I want to be able to take extended periods away from my business, either with my family or on my own, without the business being negatively impacted.

➤ I know I want to grow and develop as a leader, but I am unsure how to do this.

➤ I want to build a senior leadership team that both challenges and supports me as we scale the business to the next level, but I am nervous about this next step.

If one or more resonate with you, then read on. By the end of the book you will have:

➤ discovered the secret way of reframing your relationship with your business

➤ understood how to adopt a different mindset that will be more appropriate for the next stage of your business journey

➤ been introduced to the specific components, elements and attributes you will need to embed into your business in order to reach maturity.

Before we get started, I need to suggest that to extract the maximum value from this book you should be 100 per cent honest with yourself about where you currently are as a leader and the current state of your business. The more honest you are, and the more time you spend reflecting on yourself, the better the proposed solutions will work. A deeper realisation and a better understanding will enable you to make the required changes needed with confidence and clarity, which will increase the probability of success.

Who is this book for?

This book is for anyone involved in leading a business, more specifically including the following:

➤ **Current CEOs/MDs of private companies** – I know how lonely it can be at the top of the organisation chart, when you are trying to work through multiple challenges, especially if you don't have a critical friend or a trusted advisor to bounce concerns, ideas and thoughts off.

➤ **C-level executives working for ambitious CEOs/MDs** – in some ways being one step down in the organisation chart is a more challenging position than leading, as you have pressures to absorb from both above and below. You probably want to be the one at the top in the future, but currently lack the exposure to all aspects of the business to fully comprehend what is needed.

➤ **A leader of a not-for-profit (NFP) organisation** – whether you are leading a commercial or NFP organisation, 90 per cent of the challenges are the same and you need to be every bit as much an inspirational leader as your commercial counterpart.

How to use this book

The book can be broken down into three sections.

Chapters 1 to 3 – why you might be feeling either frustrated, underwhelmed or both

These chapters focus on the specific challenges facing leaders in high-growth businesses. Specifically, I articulate why success may feel slightly underwhelming or disappointing. I address the root cause of the misalignment between expectations and reality before suggesting where the solution may lie. I recommend you read these chapters first before moving on to the later chapters, and if necessary re-read to fully absorb the ideology and concepts presented as these are the foundations for the transformation I am encouraging you to make.

Chapters 4 to 9 – where to focus time and energy to make the transformation required

These chapters describe the six critical components that differentiate an adolescent, dependent-based business from an autonomous mature company. This is the heart of the book and in each chapter I explain how the way you view and organise each specific component needs to change and develop if your business is going to move on to the next level.

Each component has three essential elements that are the behaviours and actions needed to make change happen.

These chapters can be read in the order they are presented, or you may prefer to dive into them depending on which you value most. Either way, you ideally need each of the six critical components present in your business, so it is important that you not only comprehend each component, but also understand their relationship to each other. As businesses scale it is essential they become less departmentalised and more collaborative in the way they operate. These components are applicable across an organisation and are reliant upon inter-departmental teamworking for them to be successfully adopted.

Chapter 10 – where to start

The final section is about what needs to happen first and the choices you have to make. As a coach, trainer and facilitator, I get the opportunity to ask questions, articulate ideas and demonstrate best practice, but in the end, it is down to the recipients to put this into action. The contents of this book are no different. I sincerely hope that you will be encouraged, motivated, coaxed, challenged, or a combination of all four, into making some changes to the way you lead your business.

Reflect and commit

You will find at the end of each chapter a short section called 'Reflect and commit'. This is to encourage you to pause at the end of each chapter and to think about how the content and ideas put forward in that chapter can be applied to your own situation. Do my experiences and views resonate with your own situation? And if so, what can you do to change some of the elements that aren't working for you at present? *I want this book to generate action and not just stimulate your thinking.* Thinking is necessary as the first step, but unless action is taken nothing will change.

My aim is that you will gain the clarity, the conviction and the confidence to become a better version of yourself and simultaneously your business can become a better version of its current form. I believe that when it comes to success there doesn't have to be a gap between expectations and reality. As human beings we have the cognitive ability to make conscious choices, so if we choose each day to better ourselves, all other factors being equal, the gap between our expectations and our reality will close day by day. The choice is ours.

My recommendation to you is to dive straight into Chapters 1 and 2 before another project or task distracts you. I know you are busy, but I also know from personal experience, unless you take immediate action and start to take on board the themes and ideas put forward, there is a risk that it won't happen.

I promise you after reading those chapters you will be clearer both on why success doesn't feel as good as you thought it would, and why it is not entirely your fault that you feel the way you currently do.

You can start to transform your business now: just turn to the next page.

1. Unfulfilled Expectations

A moment of clarity
The realisation

Apparently, everyone has a book inside them, and the theory goes that we are all just waiting for a catalyst or the right time to write it. While I am not sure I entirely agree with that point of view, I do know that for me there was a particular conversation I had with a client that dramatically increased my motivation towards creating this book.

I had been working with this particular client for just over 12 months and had been confiding in him about my desire to write a book around my coaching philosophy and beliefs. He shared with me how his relationship with his business had changed since he had been working with me as his coach. He had just returned from a memorable family holiday to Lapland – which previously would have been unattainable due to his over-commitment to his business. He realised while on a husky-led sleigh ride how over the past year he had significantly changed his role in the business. Previously, he had been taking the role of the lead husky dog, out in front setting the pace for the business, taking the strain, without really knowing how hard people were working behind him. He had a very poor view of what the future terrain looked like, no great view of where they were heading and whether they even had enough resources to get there.

Roll on 12 months and, for the first time, he now felt like the sleigh driver. In control of both the destination and the speed of travel, with a clear view of how well his team was working, benefitting from a viewpoint which enabled him to see the obstacles and challenges they needed to overcome. At that moment, while far away from the business and enjoying quality time with his family, he was able to see what a personal transformation he had made and how his relationship with his business had changed. He had simultaneously regained control yet managed to remove himself from the day-to-day responsibility and pressure that had overwhelmed him before. It had been a good year!

On reflection, I realised that his experience as the lead husky was a very common one across the clients I had worked with, and how I wanted to assist as many business leaders as possible in seeing a different way of working with and relating to the businesses they had created. Hence this book.

Considerations
Unfulfilled expectations
Is this it?

In simple terms, if we can say delight exists when our reality exceeds expectations and happiness can be defined as reality meeting expectations, by the same logic frustration exists when the reality fails to meet expectations. Sadly for a lot of business leaders, frustration can be a daily occurrence, which then becomes their default state if no intervention or change in mindset takes place.

My aim here is to assist you in realising that *this* isn't *it*. With *this* being your current reality, and *it* being your future potential.

Growth in both a personal and business context is a choice. We consciously or subconsciously make that choice every day via our thoughts, actions, and interactions. If you don't like your current environment, then you have the power to change it. Before we go into the 'how', I want to highlight three considerations you need to be aware of that impact your personal potential, and therefore business growth.

1. Your predisposed mindset
You are wired differently

Apparently the one good thing about being a pessimist is that you are never going to be disappointed in life, as your expectations will always be either met or exceeded. On the converse side, being an optimist means that sometimes events or experiences are going to fail to live up to your expectations, which can result in anything from mild disappointment to something far stronger. Now, given that most entrepreneurs by nature are card-carrying members of life's optimists' club, it stands to reason that sometimes they are going to have times in their lives when their expectations have not been met and they feel frustrated.

An optimistic mindset is certainly one of the essential traits needed by those leading a business. If you are not confident that the business can achieve its targets, objectives and vision, the likelihood of doing so is greatly reduced.

However, while having an optimistic tendency makes it more likely that you are going to become an entrepreneur in the first place, this mindset also has its drawbacks that need to be managed if you are going to enjoy the journey you have embarked upon.

The question you need to consider is whether you are bringing the level of optimism and ambition that you are naturally comfortable with, or whether you are adopting a more realistic mindset because of the people you have around you. Are they being encouraged to raise their expectations to match yours or are you being persuaded to lower your expectations to match theirs?

The conclusion? Being different from most people and being unreasonable is OK. In fact it is arguably a prerequisite to reaching the next level.

2. Misaligned viewpoints
Other people don't see what you see

For ambitious leaders there can be a continual sense of frustration at play. This sense of frustration can often be present, even at times when from the outside everything seems to be going OK for both you and your business. From other people's viewpoint you can be judged as being a success in both financial terms and in the size of business you have created, but this does not necessarily resonate or align with your own view. This is because as an entrepreneur you are wired differently from most of the population, you play by different rules and hold yourself to higher standards. You have a yearning for creating a bigger business, for gaining more market share, for being seen as a thought leader within your chosen sector or holding a range of other aspirational ambitions that drive you on a daily basis. It is quite probable that from the perspective of everyone who works with you, the business you have created is working well with steady growth, an ever-increasing customer base and an established brand reputation, but in your own mind you know that you could be doing a lot better or growing a lot quicker.

The mindset you possessed as the entrepreneur, who maybe started this business, needs to come back to the fore if you are going to scale the business to its full potential. Procrastination and comfort are traits you need to overcome at this stage in your business evolution, as they will be encouraging you to stay as you are and carry on growing organically. Without new impetus and organisational change, you will start to experience declining profitability as costs rise faster than turnover and as competitors start to copy your one-time differentiators. The chances are you will start to lose market share and experience a flattening-out of your profit graphs. You realise this, but may have not yet verbalised this concern to others, as you may not be sure what the alternative options look like, or what to specifically do to make the transformational change that is needed.

The challenge faced by most business leaders is that they are able to see things differently from the rest of the company, as they possess a clearer vision of what is possible and also a clearer sense of what is missing. The challenge is how do you create the urgency required to change, when other people are possibly not seeing the same opportunities and challenges you are?

The conclusion? You need to become a persuasion ninja who has the superpower to enable others to see what they see (more about how you do this later in the book).

3. Fear
It's omnipresent, deal with it

A major factor that impacts us in either a positive or negative way is fear. Society in general and your team specifically may perceive leaders as a fearless breed of go-getting individuals, but the reality is very different. We all must cope with a certain amount of fear, whether we call it something less dramatic than this, or whether we name it as what it is. This fear can come in different forms, but normally falls into one of two categories: the fear of failure and the fear of success.

The majority of leaders experience fear of failure when their businesses are in the start-up or infancy stages. It might be a fear that comes from their belief that if they don't keep driving the organisation forward, at the rate they previously have, others will catch up or overtake. This fear is the same one that fuelled them during the initial phases when they weren't sure the business was going to make it and is based around the primeval 'fight or flight' reflex. Every week there is a struggle mentally around whether they are going to make it through.

As your company grows, the fear of failure remains present, but at this stage it is also likely to be joined by a fear of success. This fear is related to whether you have in place a strong enough organisation to graduate to, and prosper at, the next level. Will further success expose the weaknesses, shortcuts and misalignments that all businesses have to a degree? Will this all come tumbling down around you?

Simultaneously, you may also be fearful of your abilities as the leader to front and lead the organisation you're aiming to create.

➤ What happens if we grow much bigger?

➤ How will I cope with a larger team and more perceived responsibility?

➤ Am I going to be found as an ineffective leader at the next level?

➤ Can I develop as a leader at the same or, ideally, at a quicker rate than the organisation is growing?

➤ Do I have the business acumen necessary to run a more complex organisation?

The conclusion? Fear (or at least uncertainty) is natural. If you are not feeling somewhat fearful then you are probably playing it safe. Just embrace it and appreciate this means you are entering a personal and organisational growth phase.

Underlying challenges
Are you addressing the root causes enough?

Once you have got comfortable with the considerations that accompany future growth there are five additional underlying challenges that can potentially becalm a leader. This becalming means their business will remain an adolescent one until these challenges are overcome.

They may not all be present for you currently, as you may have addressed some of them already. However, the presence of at least one can have a negative impact on the confidence and clarity you need to lead your organisation on to the next level, resulting in stagnation.

Sometimes it is not simply a case of being able to eliminate the challenges that you are facing in totality before you can move forward. Initially it may be a case that you just need to acknowledge that they are present. Some may need further exploration and consideration before you can act. One of the aims of this book is to encourage you as a leader to spend more time on self-discovery and increase your own self-awareness. I feel very strongly that before you jump into action, you need to understand the situation well enough, to make sure the action you propose is the most appropriate path to take and not just the first one that you thought of.

The first stage is just to read through and consider each of these potential growth obstacles and reflect on whether they apply to you. You may need to acknowledge their presence initially and get comfortable being uncomfortable for a while before you move into the resolution phase.

1. Overcoming limiting beliefs
Can you get out of your own way?

Limiting beliefs operate either consciously or subconsciously within us all. Their mere presence can prevent us from being more proactive, more daring, and a truer version of our selves.

A limiting belief is one that constrains us in some way. Our commitment to these beliefs stops us from thinking, acting or verbalising against them. Therefore their very presence inhibits our growth as individuals and reduces our quality of life. These limiting beliefs can be focused on our own abilities, our self-identity, or even the way we see the world in general. Irrespective of their area of focus, they impact our daily thoughts, actions and deeds. They prevent us becoming the best version of our selves.

Back in the heyday of explorers, a widely held limiting belief was that the world was flat and that if you travelled too far in one direction you would fall off the edge. As ridiculous as this now sounds, you can imagine the presence of this belief limited the distances people were willing to travel. This continued until someone challenged this belief and proved that the world was in fact round. Once this limiting belief was replaced with an opposing fact, travelling great distances became possible for those keen to broaden their horizons.

Limiting beliefs in a business context

In a business context, limiting beliefs generally shows up in two areas, either in relation to your leadership or to the organisation's scalability.

1. Limiting leadership-based beliefs:

These are sometimes related to a leader's own ability with a specific function of their business such as:

➤ I am not good with numbers.

➤ I am unconfident at creating processes and systems.

➤ I need to be meeting all new customers personally.

Or around their self-identity as the leader of the business:

➤ I am not a great communicator.

➤ I am not skilled enough to lead at the next level (the fear of success in play).

➤ I am not a creative thinker.

2. Limiting beliefs that exist in relation to the future scalability of the business as a whole:

These can be around the people:

➤ We can't find the right quality of people.

➤ We can't afford to hire better quality people.

➤ We need to continue operating in a familiar way – it worked until now.

Or around businesses, customers or clients:

➤ They won't be able to afford to pay a higher price.

➤ They are always complaining, whatever we do.

➤ The customer is always right.

Or around the external market and conditions the business operates in:

➤ We are best sticking to the market we know.

➤ Given the overall economic conditions it is the wrong time to expand.

➤ We haven't the time to commit to research and development, producing new offerings.

If these concerns are left unaddressed and unchallenged, they will inhibit performance. Leaders will find themselves crafting strategies and implementing tactics on the false premises that their limiting beliefs bring into play. Without the awareness to know what is real and what is perceived, leadership can become erratic and confusing to those being led. For an organisation or individual to achieve their full potential, limiting beliefs need to be challenged head-on and overcome.

How to overcome a limiting belief – a 6-step process

Step 1 – Isolate
Recognise the existence of the belief and isolate it. When you catch yourself thinking or acting in a limited belief mindset, and then make sure you understand what is at the root cause of that belief.

Step 2 – Find the source
Think back to when this belief was formed and what evidence/circumstances existed to create it. Was it something you were told or was it something you experienced?

Step 3 – Commit to change
Acknowledge that this once may or may not have been true, but that the past does not equal the future. One bad experience of public speaking, for instance, doesn't make you a bad public speaker. It could be that you just didn't prepare well enough for your previous experience, or you didn't know the audience well enough. Both are factors that you can change before your next attempt.

Step 4 – Empowering belief
In the same way as limiting beliefs constrain performance, empowering beliefs can expand performance. All you need to do is create a belief so that the opposite outcome can be true. In the same way visualisation creates a positive experience in the brain and creates a memory of success even before any physical action has taken place, an empowering belief will nullify the impact of the limiting belief over time.

Step 5 – Visualisation
Think through the implication of this sentence: 'What if my previous thought wasn't true?'

➤ How would your business or your life be better?

➤ What if you could recruit great people into your business who were as motivated for success as you are?

➤ What if you could spend time understanding your financials so you can confidently expand your business?

Creating positive future outcomes will encourage you to take action towards creating a new belief. You need to picture success and then work towards that.

Step 6 – Embedding
To embed this new empowering belief, you need to focus on the things that need to be true for this belief to materialise. You need to find evidence of success that proves that this could be possible. In the example of public speaking, think about an occasion when you spoke well in public. It might have only been to a small group, but it is evidence that contradicts your previously held limiting belief, so focus on it. Create a positive mantra you can repeat to yourself regularly and create opportunities to practise and get better. Your performance in this area will constantly improve, reinforcing your new empowering belief.

A continual process

This process of replacing limiting beliefs with empowering beliefs is a continual mission for those of us seeking to improve and develop ourselves. In a business context this process can be magnified across the whole company, in a way that creates a very solution-focused, positive thinking, proactive organisation. Alternatively, you are left with an organisation that stagnates, questions its ability and limits its own growth potential.

The key ingredient in my experience is the collective mindset at the top of the organisation. As any organisation grows it is going to come across different challenges and circumstances from those it has previously experienced. So it is essential that those leading the business meet these challenges with a positive mindset, and that limiting beliefs don't accumulate alongside the challenges actually preventing growth.

Are your limiting beliefs getting in the way of your addressing the 'actual' challenges your business needs to solve?

2. Committing to autonomy
Letting go to gain more control

The next challenge – once you have reframed some of those limiting beliefs that have been knowingly or subconsciously preventing you moving forward – is to actually walk your talk. It is easy to tell ourselves a story about how things are going to be different in the future, but the reality of living up to this personal commitment can be a lot more challenging for some leaders than others.

You can probably admit to yourself that you are still spending too much time focusing on the operational aspects of the business. Moving out of this space, and spending more time working on future opportunities and strategies, is a constant challenge. One of the reasons this is so tough is because your focus and drive on the operational side has created the business that you have before you. Therefore moving away from this and handing this responsibility to someone else who might never have quite your drive or experience makes this hard to do. However, this move to a creative visionary role is the change you need to make if you are going to transition from an adolescent business dependent on the owner-operator (leader) to an autonomous company which runs independently from your direct input.

Moving out of the operational space will automatically create a void that will need to be filled initially by your senior leadership team, and eventually by your middle-level managers. If you don't move, they will get frustrated by the lack of career progression and what they may perceive as a lack of confidence in them, resulting in them looking for personal progression elsewhere.

The changes that need to take place are illustrated in figures (i) and (ii) below. As you will see in figure (i) there is an overload in the bottom left-hand corner of the matrix (operations/logic) and an absence of any leadership time in the opposite quadrant (strategy/creative). Basically, everyone is covering the same ground in the same way a bunch of five-year-olds will spend the majority of their first few football matches just chasing the ball, giving no thought to where to position themselves tactically! You can imagine throwing a metaphorical blanket over the enthusiastic footballers; the same blanket can cover the activities of the MD/SLT/managers in a lot of adolescent companies.

*i. What currently happens inside **adolescent** stage companies?*

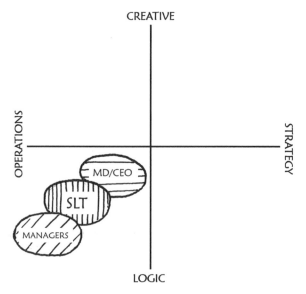

This contrasts with a mature stage company in figure (ii) where there is an obvious and defined gap between the positions of the three groups of leaders/managers. This results in greater accountability and progression for the managers and senior leadership team. At the same time, it gives the CEO a greater amount of freedom and creative space to get back to being the entrepreneurial person who created the company in the first instance.

ii. What happens inside *mature* stage companies

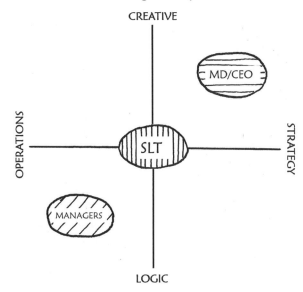

Time Frame Focus	Adolescents	Mature
MD/CEO	This month	Next year
SLT	This week	This year
Managers	Today	This quarter

The other factors that change with this more balanced approach are the time frame each group works to and the horizons they reach for. The change in focus allows for time frames to be altered, with more time being allocated to future opportunities rather than just focussing on current challenges.

You can see how this commitment to autonomy has direct and indirect consequences for the MD in particular, but also for the organisation as a whole.

Do you just like the idea of an autonomous organisation or are you really prepared to commit to creating one?

3. Transformation not tinkering is required
Are you being honest with yourself?

To reach the adolescent stage of the business growth curve most companies will have followed an evolutionary approach. They have adapted and changed when new challenges and situations have arisen. Since they are relatively small and agile, this approach is both appropriate and easy to implement.

The harder challenge occurs when adolescent stage businesses try to reach maturity, as there are so many more factors to consider when the business is both bigger and more complex. At this point the leaders have a critical choice to make over the type of change they feel is most appropriate to progress to the next level. The choices are laid out in the matrix in the figure below.

As you will see there is a choice to be made here and leaders don't have to accept or settle for gradual improvements. Do they follow a transformative change programme, or do they just choose a little realignment? Will incremental changes be enough to keep ahead of the competition (or in some cases catch up with the market leaders) or is a more radical (Big Bang) approach needed?

Classification of change
Change can be classified by the extent of the change required, and the speed with which the change is to be achieved:

LEVEL OF TRANSFORMATION

		CHANGE	ADJUSTMENT
RATE OF TRANSFORMATION	INCREMENTAL	**Revision:** Transformational change which is introduced over a period of time in inter-related areas of the business.	**Rethinking:** Steps taken to realign a businesses operational processes, in a number of stages.
	RAPID	**Total transformation:** A major shift occurs simultaneously across a number of initiatives, this is likely a reactive change due to new competitive conditions.	**Repositioning:** Adjustments are undertaken within many initiatives simultaneously, again this is likely due to a change in competitive context.

There are two inherent dangers present here, depending on which level of change you choose. If you select incremental change there is a danger that you don't change enough and that the organisation doesn't maintain or improve its market position, profitability and/or turnover. You gradually lose whatever core competencies and competitive advantages you once had and the organisation stagnates or, worse still, declines. On the other hand, if you choose the more radical 'Big Bang' option, the inherent danger is that your stakeholders (customers, employees and shareholders) can't cope with or fund the level of change that you experience. The amount of change creates turmoil and uncertainty, which leads to confusion about who you are as a company.

The major difference between the two approaches is the level of proactivity and impact the leadership team can have over the process. In the evolutionary option their role is reactionary and their impact is less significant, whereas in a revolutionary approach the onus rests on them to be proactive and to lead the change process. The former is largely an externally dictated process, whereas the latter is internally controlled.

The truth is most businesses are further along the growth curve than they appreciate, which means that they can react too slowly. They are still too reliant on lag rather than lead metrics, which means trends are being picked up too late. It is also true that consumer habits (both B2C and B2B) change quicker than ever before, produced by more choice and lower switching costs. Therefore there is an imperative for the leader to be 100 per cent honest with themselves about the current state of the business. This must happen before they can choose the required level of change.

Are you being realistic in your assessment of your current business, your team and your offering, or just trying to be a popular leader?

4. The distraction of overwhelm
Are you busy being busy or busy being productive?

One of my favourites quotes is from the 19th century US philosopher and poet Henry David Thoreau that simply states: *'It's not enough to be busy; so are the ants. The question is: what are we busy about?'*

This quote resonates with me for two reasons. First, when I was running my own SMEs I can remember spending all day putting out fires and responding to other people's requests without really achieving much that moved the business forward. Second, I don't think I have come across a business leader yet that wouldn't claim to be constantly busy and have too little time to achieve their aims. The sad aspect of this busyness and extinguishing of operational-level fires is ultimately that neither are satisfying nor fulfilling. It may give you short-term satisfaction, but like a caffeine fix the impact soon wears off. For those leading a rapidly expanding adolescent business, it is very easy to get caught in this type of work and not allocate enough time to important or strategic work.

With the benefit of hindsight, I realise now that allowing myself to focus on operational-level tasks was partially an avoidance tactic and partially symptomatic of not possessing the mindset to shift to a different way of working. What I was avoiding was trading work I understood and could definitely complete (putting out operational fires and feeling like a hero) for work that I was unsure of and didn't have the confidence to perform properly (strategic planning and implementation). The mindset shift I needed was to realise that other people could learn how to put out the fires and do the operational-level work as well as I could, even if their approach was slightly different. I needed to acknowledge that if I didn't focus time and energy on the important strategic work it just wouldn't get done. No one else had either the ability or more importantly the reason to do this work. The operational work was not important but urgent. My role was to focus on the work that was both important and urgent. This principle underpins the logic behind the Eisenhower Decision-Making Matrix illustrated below:

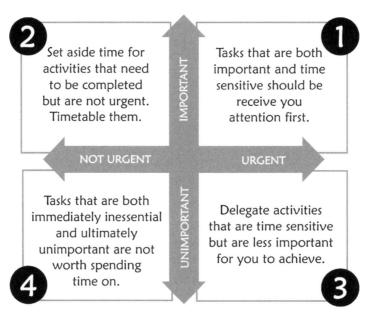

(This version of US president Dwight D. Eisenhower's decision-making strategy is adapted from www.papergazer.com)

Your role as a business leader is to spend most time on Box 1. By doing so you will reduce the sense of overwhelm you get from spending too much of your time on tasks from the other three boxes. However, to make this change you need to accept that other leaders in the business are going to get more attention and perceived importance in the eyes of both your employees and customers. There is a paradox at play here: to get the business to where you are currently it has needed to be centred around you, but to move the business to the next level it can't be all about you. This is the mental shift that will allow the business to transform from dependency to autonomy. You need to maintain a high degree of influence, but simultaneously reduce the amount of direct input. Only by accepting this change will you be able to move from overwhelm to a state of more control and focus, where you have the time and space to do the strategic work both your company and your role require you to do.

Is your default state the inspirational leader or an operational-level manager?

5. The fear of the unknown vs the ennui of the status quo
Time for a leap of faith

Conscious decision-making

One of the attributes that has enabled human beings to remain the dominant species on earth is our ability to make conscious decisions. Conscious thought is deliberate as opposed to the reactionary instincts used by less evolved species. Given that it is obviously a positive attribute it is surprising how much of our lives are spent operating on autopilot with no real decision-making taking place, just preset patterns of behaviour being rolled out day after day. This can be particularly true in business settings where a large majority of the working population receive a wage for exhibiting a pre-agreed set of behaviours and actions for eight hours a day. Both parties (the company and the employee) accept this situation as it gives a satisfactory outcome for both parties. This aligns with the analysis of Tony Robbins, one of the most highly regarded life coaches. He suggests certainty is one of a set of basic human needs. However, too much certainty can lead to boredom and can stifle creativity.

What high performance companies have discovered is that if you can create a workplace where conscious decision-making is present and championed, then employees are more engaged. This higher level of employee engagement results in increased performance and higher employee retention.

We as business leaders get to choose and decide the type of company we set up, the hours we operate, the ways we operate, the ways we remunerate, etc. The higher performing companies make sure they are constantly evaluating all of these to create the most desirable combination to best fit the needs of their key stakeholders (their team members, their customers and their shareholders). If we take it one step further, the truly great companies have created an infrastructure that positively allows and encourages the various stakeholders to be part of this process. The pyramid-shaped organisational structure, with all decisions being taken at the top and then filtered down to the rest of the company as preset processes and non-negotiable policies, is no longer fit for purpose (and arguably never was).

A new relationship with your business

These changes in mindset and ideally infrastructure provide the opportunity for a more fundamental change to take place: the relationship you have with your business. While the business is establishing (the infancy stage) and then growing (the adolescence stage) it is understandable, and probably even necessary, for the entrepreneur leader to personally drive the business forward. They need to invest most of their time and energy to get the business first established and then profitable. During these phases it is a very personal relationship, with every success and every failure being taken personally by the leader – an emotional roller coaster in many respects. While this behaviour pattern and relationship with the business may seem desirable, or at least appear necessary, there are two potentially negative outcomes generated.

First, this type of relationship is very tiring, both physically and mentally, so it's difficult to sustain. Additionally, as energy levels drop, the probability is that the performance of the business will follow the same downward curve or at the very least grow more slowly. This can be compared to a marathon runner who starts a race too quickly and by the time they realise their mistake they have spent all their energy.

The second negative outcome is that this very personal relationship can have a negative impact on the relationship other team members have with the business. Without realising it, the leader may disempower others from becoming as passionate as they are about the business. Their own level of commitment and passion can be intimidating or alienating to their employees, who cannot contribute at the level they would like to. They may feel they cannot match the leader's standards or level of emotional investment and consequently become less motivated.

Therefore the shift needed here is for the leader to move from operating *in* their business and being the centre (and often therefore the bottleneck) of every decision and process, to a position where they spend a greater percentage of their time working *on* their business. As referenced earlier in this book, my client's transition from being lead husky to the sleigh driver is a good example of someone who has managed to successfully make this transformation.

Unless this shift happens then it is very unlikely the business will ever reach maturity and optimise the potential return for its shareholders. The irony is that in many cases the owner-operator (or leader) may be one of the largest shareholders at this point, so their behaviour and re-positioning of their own relationship with the business is a key determinator of the level of return they see on their own investment. Unless they 'the leader' make a shift, they 'the shareholder' are going to be short-changed.

Letting go to gain real control

Admittedly, this can be a very difficult concept for leaders to process, as it feels counterintuitive in many ways. But if you look at serial entrepreneurs more closely, you will see the only way they can achieve a level and consistency of success over multiple businesses is to adopt this mindset from day one. They are not afraid to bring in people that know more than them about the particular industry or role function within the business. Plus they never get too involved with the day-to-day operations, meaning that the delivery of the service or product is never dependent on their personal input. This means that others must not only take on a higher degree of personal responsibility very early on in the business life cycle, but also this allows for much more objectivity when regarding the performance of the business. Therefore less emotive and more commercially based decisions are made as the business grows.

If the dependency phase lasts too long it becomes much harder to change and doesn't end up benefitting either the business or the leader. In the same way, if an adolescent offspring remains dependent on its parents, this is an unhealthy state for both parties. If a leader stays too long in the centre of the business, the business becomes too dependent on their input to grow and mature at its true potential speed.

The leap of faith needed here, to move from the known to the unknown, is the crux of this book.

Do you want to run an adolescent, dependent business or a mature, independent one?

Key takeaways
Summary

Realising there may be a better way to operate that could serve both you and your business is the first step. Like any transformation programme, acknowledging the necessity for change is step one; acknowledge the underlying factors that currently hold you back. Moving forward, you must have the openness to consider a range of potentially counterintuitive solutions; this will enable you to reposition your role in, and relationship with, your business. This is challenging work, but the rewards are high for those willing to undertake it.

Reflect and commit

Before you move on to the next chapter, I would encourage you to spend time reflecting on the five underlying challenges, to consider if any of these currently apply to you and your business:

1   Are there any limiting beliefs negatively impacting your performance as a leader?

2   Are you consciously or unconsciously resisting letting go of areas of the business that could be performed equally well by others?

3   Are you thinking too small about the extent of change needed to move your business to the next level?

4   Are you spending too much time working IN the business rather than ON the business, resulting in a sense of overwhelm?

5   Are you being honest enough with yourself about the state of your business and the impact this is having on you?

Now based on those reflections, what are you prepared to commit to change?

I will start...
I will stop...
I will do more...
I will do less...

What's next?
Conflicting needs

Now we have identified the overall challenges, the next chapter will start to explore what should be in place at the centre of the organisation to enable this transformation to take place. You will also be introduced to the central themes I believe you need to embed to enable your business to scale further with confidence and clarity.

2. Conflicting Needs

Overview

Rethinking success criteria

Looking back to when I was running my own SMEs, I now realise that I was quantifying success incorrectly. In simple terms, I was judging success as numerical output and not considering what that output was worth to others. At the time I wasn't as successful as I had hoped to be, if I am using that primitive output measurement to judge success. But on further reflection, if I consider the impact on others such as my employees (what they went on to achieve), my customers (what they gained from the businesses) and the community (how my businesses added experiences and opportunities that weren't there before), I can now view my success very differently.

It comes down to balancing conflicting needs. There are your personal needs, the needs of your various stakeholders and the needs of the wider community you operate within. You get to choose which you focus on and which ultimately you manage to satisfy. Ideally you would like to simultaneously satisfy all of these, but in reality that can become challenging as growth often puts some needs in conflict with each other.

In this chapter, I explore why these conflicting needs pose such a challenge and propose a set of frameworks that you can adopt to enable you to reframe the challenge and balance them effectively.

1. A mantra to ingrain: *better before bigger*

Are you prioritising correctly?

As a society we can be very size obsessed. We have become very judgemental around size as opposed to quality, to the detriment of the latter. Meals are sold in super sizes and cars have become twice as large they were before. Bigger is generally accepted as better from a consumer and market perspective. As business leaders we can easily get caught in the same trap that leads us to talk about our business in relation to size metrics (turnover, head count, etc.), rather than quality metrics (Net Promoter Score, employee retention rate). This obsession, if not acknowledged and checked, means that we can end up focusing on growth for growth's sake without taking quality into account. Quality is more difficult to measure and less definable, but I believe it underpins growth. If the quality is not high enough, the growth will ultimately tail off and, in the most severe cases, stop altogether, leading ultimately to the failure of the business as a going concern.

One concept, if not the key one, I am suggesting to facilitate the transition from adolescence to maturity is a prioritisation on *better before bigger*. This standpoint may oppose your current philosophy, but it is paramount to enable your company the transform. Here are the reasons why.

i. Honest conversations required

Leaders rely on a variety of indicators to make decisions and form opinions. Most of these decisions are tangible, made up of data and narratives brought to them or their external consultants. The danger here is leaders not digging deep enough or asking enough challenging questions of their direct reports. This can result in them being 'led' rather than 'leading'.

To lead, it is essential to have the quality and depth of conversations around the indicators to understand whether the current strategy and tactics are giving the required quality as well as quantity outcomes. These outcomes must meet both the short-term and more importantly the long-term goals of the company. You need to know the narrative behind the headline number.

The key to diving deep enough and leading, rather than being led, is simply to have enough honest conversations across the company. As the leader you naturally have an 'access all areas' pass, but are you using that privilege well enough? When was the last time you had coffee with one of your front-line staff, who spends most of their time dealing with your customers, to understand how well the customer interface is actually working? When was the last time you engaged properly with your accounts department, to understand the challenges they face because of the increased volume of business? And when was the last time you spoke with a selection of customers, to really understand what it is like to do business with your company?

If you are going to truly transform your company, it would pay to spend enough time and dive deep enough with your 'due diligence' phase first. This will make sure the information reported to you is the whole truth. Additionally, this will make sure that you understand the depth of the challenges you face as a company. The due diligence I am encouraging you to undertake here serves to triangulate the data and reports with some human-to-human conversations across your company; together you are getting a complete appraisal of the status quo.

If you are going to take the time and invest the required money to create a business that you can confidently scale to the next level, then you need to start with a deep enough, and wide enough, personal understanding of the current state of the business.

ii. Are you achieving the twin goals of increasing volume and increasing quality?

Businesses are often viewed on a one-dimensional basis, where we simply plot a chosen metric against time to judge whether we are progressing at the desired speed and with the desired trajectory. This approach can work for a while, but without a corresponding measurement around the quality of what you are producing, this type of analysis is fundamentally flawed. It is too simplistic to demonstrate whether you will be able to continue and ideally increase the level of profitability within the business. This, of course, is the primary objective of all private companies.

In reality, businesses need to constantly be measuring volume (numbers of units produced/sold, etc.) and quality (satisfaction levels, repeat buys, etc.). If we think of this as a classic 2x2 matrix it would look like the figure overleaf:

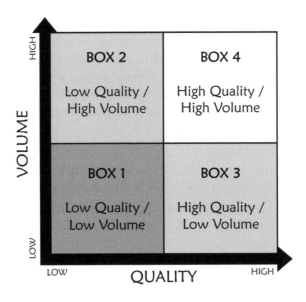

The Volume/Quality Matrix

Now, it is obvious that most businesses aspire to Box 4 as the ideal scenario; and interestingly most will approach Box 4 via Box 2, rather than via Box 3. This means that they have moved from the undesirable and unsustainable Box 1 by focusing on increasing volume, rather than increasing quality. Now this is a very simplistic statement, symptomatic of working from a 2x2 matrix, but in my experience it tends to be the norm. Most businesses focus on having just enough quality to enable them to increase the volume, rather than focusing on improving the quality to a level that will naturally increase the volume.

This strategic choice has been made primarily because this seems the easier option. Once you have a 'good enough' offering (good enough being measured either against competitor's offerings or from customer feedback) the natural inclination is to turn the taps on and increase the volume of that offering. The danger with this strategy is that it is difficult to defend. You are exposed to competition from a well-resourced competitor, who can offer a lower price point for a similar offering. By focusing your strategy on volume and selling the most in your chosen market you are gambling on becoming one of the biggest players in your market and, critically, being able to maintain that position.

The alternative is to create a quality offering that differentiates you, for which you can charge a premium price. Moving to Box 3 rather than Box 2 will mean you don't necessarily need to be the biggest player in your market as you have a premium offering with a high profit margin.

For example, Ferrari need to sell far fewer cars per year than Fiat as their margins are so much higher; they focus on being the best option in their market rather than the biggest.

Leaders of adolescent stage businesses have a clear strategic decision to make. Do you want to focus on being the best or being the biggest? Being perceived as the best will probably result in your being one of the biggest, but the reverse is not often true. Being big for the sake of it won't necessarily give you a sustainable competitive advantage.

iii. Clear blue waters desired

The mantra of getting *better before bigger* is based on the premise that people judge you, and more importantly you judge yourself, on the quality of your product. Size without quality is unsatisfying for most of us and should not define your business legacy.

So, if this applies to you, I would encourage some thought on how you might create something which enables your business to be competitive not just in your current market, but ideally to form a whole new market. Apple's iPad provided an entirely new type of gadget technology, and Henry Ford famously said, 'If I had given the public what they wanted, I would have built faster horses.'

Chan Kim and Renee Mauborgne champion the concept of 'clear blue waters' in their 2004 book *Blue Ocean Strategy*. They assert that companies should aim for and implement strategies that create a leap in the value proposition of the company. This can consequently unlock new demand within an unexplored market, and simultaneously make competition irrelevant.

Time to choose

There is an opportunity present if you are a successful adolescent stage business, to use your established platform as a launch pad for creating something far better than your current output. There are multiple challenges inherent in this strategy, like accepting growth may slow during this transformation period. However, along with the challenges, there are multiple benefits for your various stakeholders if you implement a *better before bigger* mantra. These include:

➤ less overwhelm for employees and the chance to develop new skills

➤ a maintenance (or probable) improvement in customer service

➤ a more sustainable and profitable company for shareholders.

Better before Bigger is a challenging concept for leaders who have up until now focused primarily on increasing output rather than quality; nevertheless, it is a strategic choice that I would recommend you seriously consider.

2. The paradox to manage: *flucture*

Have you the optimal amount of structure & flexibility present?

Technically, a paradoxical state is defined as the presence of two seemingly contradictory qualities in a single entity. I believe that a paradox exists at the heart of most adolescent stage businesses (the entity), and the two qualities forming the paradox are a desire to remain flexible, but a need to implement more structure. I call this the paradox of *flucture* – the name acknowledging the elements of both qualities.

There are a series of recurring questions which leaders wrestle with that demonstrate the presence of this paradox. They will sound something like these:

➤ Have we created a company strong enough to scale at the next level?

➤ Are our systems and processes defined enough and embedded to enable us to cope with further growth?

➤ Do we have enough 'quality' people to take on more leadership and accountability as we scale?

➤ Are we too customer centric, and focus too much on their needs, rather than balancing the needs of all our stakeholders?

➤ What would happen if my key team members resigned tomorrow, how would we cope?

These are difficult to definitively answer unless you spend enough time on each, and detach yourself enough to be honest about the current state of your business

The presence of two seemingly opposing properties with different attributes is initially hard to comprehend, but if we dig a little deeper, we can see how the presence of both attributes actually serves the entity.

i. Operating within a paradox

Paradoxes are omnipresent and therefore learning to operate within them is an approach which serves leaders better than trying to eliminate them.

Seeing the positive

In his book *The Age of Paradox*, the eminent business thinker Charles Handy forwards the view that because change is occurring more rapidly than ever, challenging the assumptions and traditions of previous decades, the unintended consequences of these changes cannot be solved, but must be managed. He suggests, 'There are pathways through the paradoxes if we can understand what is happening and are prepared to act differently.' The paradoxes Handy refers to are societal based, the majority of first world inhabitants having more money but seemingly less time to spend it. As well as this, the end of lifelong careers has given us the freedom to explore new opportunities but has also removed the security and comfort needed to enjoy this freedom. In conclusion, it relies on our agency to find the ideal balance point within these paradoxes.

Motivational guru Tony Robbins presents the idea of six fundamental human needs that must be satisfied for us to feel fulfilled. He believes paradoxes must be managed, rather than solved. These six needs are formed into three pairs of opposing states. The first of these pairs is the need for both certainty and uncertainty in our lives. Like Handy, Robbins suggests that the presence of both states is essential and that we should focus on achieving the optimal personal balance between them rather than attempting to remove one.

The presence of two seemingly conflicting properties with opposing attributes serves the entity (our business) in different ways without reducing the effectiveness of either attribute; in fact, the presence of these opposing properties can actually enhance the entity.

The necessity of tension

Paradoxical properties can allow our business to scale well beyond the level it might do if only one element was present. The key here is learning to live with the paradox and finding the balance point between the two. To achieve optimal performance, a healthy tension needs to exist between the two states, so one is always challenging the other.

In the Robbins example, if we have too much uncertainty and not enough certainty, we become scared. On the other hand, if we have too much certainty and not enough uncertainty, we become bored. Neither being scared or bored are desirable states, and a position somewhere between the two would be optimal for most of us. Therefore feeling both certain and uncertain simultaneously is the healthiest way to exist.

Similarly, a very structured business or business leader needs to be challenged to test whether less structure and more flexibility serve their customers better. It may even assist them in attracting more of the right type of customers. Too much structure in their strategy may result in them missing out on market sectors that could use their service or buy their products if the offering was repackaged or repositioned in a different way.

ii. Symbiosis in action – When the desire for flexibility meets the need for structure

I have coined the word *flucture* to symbolise the situations where flexibility is desired, but more structure is needed. This seemingly contrasting state can work in isolation, but on most occasions both states are improved by the presence of the other; a symbiotic relationship exists between the two. The concept of *flucture* exists in both the natural and manufactured worlds; I am recommending it should also exist in the business world.

Tall trees need strong roots

In nature trees cannot grow and maintain their height without a combination of both structure and flexibility. The roots and internal capillaries give them a strong basis and core, i.e. the structure that allows optimal growth to occur. However, they also have the ability to flex as required, to cope with climatic conditions (such as wind and storms) in order to survive. The oldest trees have been around for hundreds of years and have only been able to achieve this longevity by a combination of being in the right location with the appropriate amounts of internal structure and flexibility. In comparison, those trees that have an excess of structure won't grow very tall (or probably survive), as they don't have the necessary root system to gain great height. Meanwhile, those trees that don't have the appropriate amount of flexibility won't survive extreme conditions. Depending on their location and growth stage, there is an optimum combination of both flexibility and structure required in order for the tree to grow and prosper.

Engineers know best

Humans have copied the principles that exist in the natural world, replicating them in engineering projects. Skyscrapers and large bridges are engineered to have both structure and flexibility present. In fact, the desirability of both becomes more essential the larger the scale of the engineering project. A small bridge or building can survive, for a period, with the absence of one of these two components. However, if any scaling is needed then all larger man-made constructions need a combination of strength with the ability to flex when required in extreme atmospheric conditions, such as strong winds, to remain intact. Engineers choose materials that have the optimum combination of both factors and build in features like rollers or expandable joints to allow a degree of flexibility when required.

A good example of engineering which failed to balance these components was the original Millennium Bridge, built across the Thames. When it was originally constructed and tested with a few dozen engineers it seemed safe, but once it was commissioned and used greater volumes of people, it was found to be unstable and dangerous, with too much flexibility. It had to be closed down and more reinforcing structure was added before being rebuilt.

Increasing longevity

It makes sense to learn lessons from both nature and engineering, and apply them to our business practices if we look to achieve similar levels of growth and efficiency.

There are very few great companies out there, if any, that have achieved considerable size, amazing profitability or exceptional longevity without having a degree of flexibility in the way they operate. The great companies can adapt to new markets or new conditions more quickly and more effectively than their competitors. To do this they need to have a degree of flexibility ingrained into the way they develop and then implement, both in their strategy and their offerings.

Paradoxically, they simultaneously possess well-defined and established operational processes that underpin their ability to sustain their profitability and growth. In the same way the largest trees have the greatest root system, and the tallest skyscrapers have the deepest foundations, established companies' growth is predicated in relation to their strong structure. There is the appropriate amount of complexity and structure to ensure the resources are used effectively. The principle behind the phrase 'survival of the fittest' applies to business as well as nature.

Survival is decided by having structure and flexibility in place, but optimal performance is based on having the appropriate combination of both. The amount of each element required is the leader's decision, and this must be continually reappraised to ensure the optimal amounts of both elements are present. Optimal here is defined by two main factors: first, the level of maturity the company has reached on the business life cycle curve; second, the maturity and predictability of the market they operate within. Let me expand on how these factors impact the optimal balance.

iii. Applying the concept of *flucture*

When looking to manage the paradox of *flucture* within your business, there are three things to consider:

1 stage of life cycle curve

2 market conditions

3 a natural deficiency of evolution present in the business.

Consideration 1: Stage of business life cycle curve

Adaptation is key
In reality, the challenge for business leaders goes one stage deeper than coping with the need for these two opposing states in their business. They also need to consider that at different stages in the business growth cycle, the desired amount of each will vary.

The business growth cycle is a well-established progression as presented opposite.

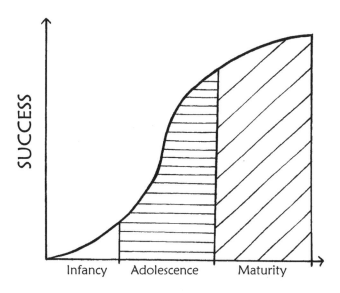

Theoretically, not all infancy businesses will succeed in achieving adolescence status, and similarly, only a small percentage of adolescent businesses will reach full maturity. Once maturity has been reached, different strategic options become available, like selling the business, or starting a new one while the initial business generates a residual income for the shareholders. The speed at which a business will progress through the different phases will vary. However, the logic behind this model suggests that, first, all businesses will need to spend a certain amount of time in each stage before progressing, and, second, that the fundamental way the business operates will need to vary at each stage to cope with its specific requirements and demands.

Infancy – When a business is starting out, it is likely that a greater degree of flexibility will be needed to create the ideal service or product, and also to find the ideal market for that service or product. The business must try different offerings, gauge the response, and repeat accordingly before finalising the initial products. This is known as the 'proof of concept' phase.

Adolescence – Once a business has progressed through infancy and is approaching adolescence, it will normally need to add more structure and process to the way it operates. This is necessary to optimise the production and delivery of the products as they aim to attract more customers and scale the business to maximise return on investment (ROI) and shareholder value within the business. They now look to dominate a market niche they have found or established for themselves.

Maturity – In the final stage, a business needs to have well-defined and ingrained processes and systems in place so that it can optimise the production and delivery of its offering. Therefore structure becomes more important than flexibility, but while flexibility plays a lesser role, it is still a crucial component for two reasons. First, there will be a continual need to create new products and services to ensure the business both retains existing clients and continues to generate more. Second, the need remains for a degree of organisational agility, so the business can react where necessary to new trends or opportunities.

The relation between the concept of *flucture* and the business life cycle stages are summarised in the chart below.

Stage of Growth	Business Life Cycle Stage		
	INFANCY	ADOLESCENCE	MATURITY
Extent	High	Moderate	Low
FLEXIBILITY	Searching for optimal product/service and ideal delivery model.	Continuing to innovate new products and services, but proof of concept emerging, and differentiators being established.	Need to focus majority of time and resources monetising most profitable offerings. Optimal ways of working have been established.
Extent	Low	Moderate	High
STRUCTURE	Little desire or time to focus on internal structures and processes.	Protocols and systems start to become ingrained as clarity emerges around ideal processes and markets.	Efficiency is paramount: increasing output and reducing cost are the two dominant drivers.

On reflection, it seems that when aiming to grow your business effectively, a paradoxical state, while initially appearing confusing and unwanted, is not only desirable but essential. This paradox helps achieve optimal performance and longevity.

Consideration 2: Market conditions

A need for more flexibility (and less structure)
A current example of an industry sector trying to become more flexible to meet the changing needs of its customers is banking. This industry has operated in a very structured way for centuries, with set procedures and protocols dictating how they should operate and react in any given situation. As a result of external changes such as increased Internet accessibility and new entrants in the market (e.g. peer-to-peer lending/ fintech companies), banks have had to become much more flexible. This is demonstrated by both the way they interact with their customers and the ranges of products and services they offer. A large percentage of banks' customers no longer visit their premises, and most will have a relationship with a number of financial institutions simultaneously. This has drastically impacted their business model, which for decades was built around personal face-to-face relationships with bank managers. These changes have forced banks to review both the way they work and how they communicate with their customers. The number of new competitors entering the market has increased as the entry requirements have continued to lessen. Consequently, banks are now having to actively compete for a share of the market, which demands both flexibility and innovation in the way they operate and create new offerings.

A desire for more structure (and less flexibility)
Conversely, too much flexibility and not enough structure may result in the loss of customers or opportunities because the market is expecting a consistent product or service. Additionally, potential customers might not understand what they will be purchasing, as every offering produced is slightly different. Hence structure within business provides the consistency needed to scale, while flexibility provides the differentiation needed to win business.

Interestingly, one example of a company that decided it had too much flexibility and innovation in the way it operated was Google. Before Larry Page took over again as CEO in 2011, they famously had a '20% initiative' throughout the company, which meant that employees were encouraged to spend 20 per cent of their time on the creation of new products and projects. However, Page decided this was counterproductive to both efficiency and profitability. He scrapped this policy to focus on fewer projects, which were more structured and governed by a sign-off policy that controlled allocated activity. Resources were being spread too thinly. While no one would say that Google's financial performance was struggling before 2011, the chart below shows that since Page's return to the helm and his changes to internal resource allocation, performance has significantly improved. In Google's case less flexibility and more structure seem to be the right combination.

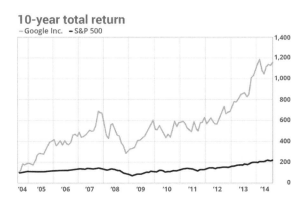

Source: FactSet.com

Consideration 3: Evolution is not naturally present

What is different about the business world?

While there are a number of similarities between nature and the business world, we should consider a couple of fundamental differences in relation to the concept of *flucture*.

First, in nature evolution has created perfectly adapted organisms that 'naturally' have the optimal degree of both structure and flexibility for their conditions. Whereas in business, these two critical components will only exist if they are embedded into the company by the leadership. The mindset and corresponding processes must be created deliberately and systematically. The earlier this is done, the more likely the organisation will flourish to its full potential. Structure is not something companies are born with; it is created by those working within them.

Second, a continual reassessment of the balance of these components is required, as the ideal proportion of each will vary based on a range of factors. These include the growth stage the business is currently in (more about this in a later chapter), or the state of the external market the business operates in. If the market is either new or subject to a high degree of change, the business may need a greater degree of flexibility in the way it operates.

Therefore while natural structures adapt and prosper through thousands of years of evolution, man-made structures or companies need continual human input to achieve the same outcome. A business without the ability to flex its strategy or resources around the needs of its customer can only survive in certain markets. Once that market has been exhausted or dries up it has nowhere to go for the resources (customers and money) it needs to survive and prosper. The obvious example here is 'bricks and mortar only' retail outlets. Historically, having a presence on the high street was a sustainable and profitable way to operate a retail business. However, as the external environment (the growth of online shopping) has changed, the retailers that have survived and prospered are those that have either combined high street and online presences successfully or those that have moved 100 per cent online. This is an example of having a sufficiently flexible business strategy that can facilitate evolution and meet customer requirements. The retailers that have prospered and expanded are those whose management developed an online ecosystem quickly or created one that aligns best with the consumer.

The importance of an effective ecosystem
If you look inside either the most profitable or the most long-lasting companies, you will find ecosystems which underpin their ability to perform at the highest level year after year. The ecosystem allows the company to continually review requirements and adapt to the changing environment it operates in. Two of the elements that are continually reviewed by the internal ecosystem are the amount of structure and flexibility required to achieve optimal performance. These companies even adopt terms like 'it's in our DNA' to reinforce the importance of these ecosystems.

So, while a plentiful supply of the fundamental resources (such as light and water for a tree, and customers and staff for a company) is essential, the presence of the resources on their own is not enough to guarantee survival. Equally essential is the presence of an internal ecosystem to control and optimise the allocation of resources, which is where structure and flexibility come into play.

The opportunity that exists

You have the opportunity to assess and adjust the critical elements of flexibility and structure in your business. Proportioning both correctly will allow you to move forward. It is not necessarily a quick or easy process to make this readjustment, but I would suggest it is worthwhile before you look to scale further. If any imbalance exists this will only be magnified once you grow further.

3. A concept to adopt:
embracing the plateau
Reflection time required

If you have ever climbed a mountain, you will appreciate there are numerous false summits that you see and reach before you finally reach the true summit. During the initial phase of the climb, you can't often see the top, as your view is obscured by the false summits.

On reaching the brow of a false summit, you experience the twin emotions of elation, for reaching what you thought was your goal, and then dejection when realising that you need to climb further to achieve your goal. Experienced mountaineers are aware of the existence of false summits and can therefore control their emotions in a way novice climbers cannot. The key is simply to embrace the plateau that is normally located next to the summit. The plateau allows for recovery; it allows you time to assess the next climb and, if you let it, gives you the vantage point to look back and celebrate your accomplishments thus far.

Plateaus are about simultaneously looking backwards and forwards. While you are climbing (or whilst your business is growing rapidly) you are often too busy dealing with the present challenges to appreciate what you have achieved so far. The plateau gives you that opportunity. I encourage all leaders to find a way of accepting and ideally embracing plateaus for what they are, and for the opportunity they present.

i. The necessity of regeneration

Being a leader can be very tiring and can also become very monotonous if you don't allow yourself the opportunity to reflect and re-energise regularly.

Embracing the plateau is an essential component if a business is going to make that leap from adolescence to maturity status. Now comes the more challenging aspect of implementation, also known as 'the how'.

The number one element of effective implementation is the emotional buy-in from the leader. Most entrepreneurs have created a business around their beliefs, values and vision. So unless the business leader adopts this mindset as a set of core beliefs, then it is very unlikely to gain the traction and support it needs to be implemented effectively across the organisation. This can't be another 'fad' or short-term fix; this needs to be a new way of operating for the foreseeable future. *Embracing the plateau* is a premeditated way of avoiding organisational burnout and needs to become part of the default company culture if sustainable growth is the goal.

The challenge that exists here is that a potential conflict may appear between what is currently working satisfactorily within the business, and the changes the leader knows are necessary to operate successfully at a higher level. It is likely that team members may not see the necessity for change in the same way the leader does. I am encouraging you to fix something that doesn't appear at first sight to be broken. An experienced marathon runner takes on fluid *before* they get thirsty; a novice waits until they feel dehydrated, which is too late to prevent a decline in performance.

In a similar way, if you wait until the cracks appear and are large enough for all stakeholders to see them, your performance will already be in (potentially terminal) decline. The time to embark on a regeneration programme is when things are going well, giving yourself more time and therefore less pressure when implementing changes.

A far-sighted and aware leader will instinctively know where upgrades are needed and will use the time on the plateau to make them. In the same way a football manager uses the off season to sign new players or embed new tactics before the start of the next season.

Thinking of your business in terms of peaks and plateaus is not easy for those leaders wedded to a diet of continual growth, but it is a more mature and sustainable concept. The alternative approach (continual growth) has a shelf-life to it, which you are probably approaching sooner than you imagine.

ii. The company-wide behaviours required

Leaders that successfully transition their company from adolescence to maturity demonstrate three specific behaviours; these must also be adopted across the business for the period of transition and ideally became part of the default culture. The desired behaviours are:

Far-sightedness. Namely the ability to stay focused on the long-term vision and not be swayed off course by shorter-term needs or demands. Decisions need to be made with the ultimate goal in mind, which may appear illogical to those focused on the short-term needs of the business.

Acceptance. The probability is that business growth and/or profitability may slow while the business goes through the necessary internal changes. Investment is made in new infrastructure and personnel, which is deemed necessary to compete at the higher level.

Courage. In the end there needs to be a 'leap of faith', albeit one based on research and data; however, there is still a step into the unknown to be taken.

Take a professional football team. A far-sighted owner/manager will know that they need better players and coaches as they move up through the divisions. They will recruit ahead of time and will have money set aside to ensure they can afford the right resources. At some point they will need to become more structured in the way they train, learn and compete if they are going to become a great team. They will start to come up against players with an equal amount of natural talent. Similarly, having a great product or service in business will get you a certain amount of success, but unless you have the required structure and attributes to differentiate you from other competing companies, your growth will stall.

A good example of this is the English golfer Nick Faldo, who decided that he needed a more structured and dependable swing in order to succeed in the major gold championships. So, despite being European number one for the previous five years, he spent 18 months learning a new way to swing. His ranking dropped initially, but once the new skill was mastered, he went on to win six major championships in the next five years and spent two years as the number one ranked golfer in the world. He was *far-sighted,* knowing that he wouldn't achieve his long-term goal without changes. He *accepted* his short-term performance would suffer, but he demonstrated the *courage* needed to take the leap of faith to make the changes and ultimately reap the reward. He appreciated that he needed to get better before he could compete successfully for the big titles.

On the flip side a very disciplined sports team that works to set structure and set plays can earn a certain amount of success. However, when they come up against an equally structured and competent team, it will be the team that can change tactics quickest or do something unexpected that is likely to prevail. Too much structure and not enough flexibility will only get you a certain amount of success in sport, as it will in business. To be a truly great business or sports team you need to have a mindset that allows you to adapt when new situations and opportunities emerge. You must have the flexibility to consider your operating position not only in relation to your opponents, but also the overall conditions (whether it is game conditions or market conditions) that you face. This mindset needs to exist throughout the team or organisation and cannot be the sole responsibility of the leader or coach. In sporting parlance this is referred to as 'playing what's in front of you', rather than sticking to the preset game plan.

iii. Tenacity is mandatory

I spent a fair portion of my adolescence running cross country and can remember my coach telling me that what I didn't possess in natural running talent, I made up for in tenacity. I basically didn't like losing, particularly as I was often running with/against my brother as one of my teammates. This was my first realisation that in life tenacity can be the mystery ingredient that levels the playing field. Tenacity allows a less-talented company (or runner) to compete with a better-resourced (or more naturally talented) rival. I would suggest this determination is a mandatory requirement for any leader embarking on a transformation programme.

To successfully implement any level of change you need clarity on the reason for change; once this has been achieved, you will then need to persuade others to align with this point of view. As we will be discussing in Chapter 4, two of the attributes inspirational leaders possess are visualisation and persuasion. A transformation programme requires the leader to be fully committed to the changes required, but they must also clearly articulate the benefits to other stakeholders. This may take time, hence tenacity being mandatory.

The right mindset across the organisation is essential if optimal business performance is going to be achieved. This mindset, as both Handy and Robbins concluded, focuses on managing the myriad of business paradoxes rather than attempting to solve them.

The 3 steps to transformation

The mantra *better before bigger*, the paradox of *flucture* and the concept of *embracing the plateau* are in their most simplistic sense the WHYs behind the need to transform. If one, or hopefully more, resonates with you, then you are entering the right mindset to lead a successful transformation programme.

The next stage of the process focuses on WHAT you need to do to this transformation. There are three steps:

Step 1: Re-confirming your organisational core
Have you re-committed to your mission, vision, and values recently?

Once you have made the commitment to organisational self-betterment, the first step of transformation is to review your previous mission, vision and values to see if they are still relevant and attainable. It may be a while since you created these documents, so the plateau phase is the perfect time to reconnect to your *why* (your mission), your *what* (your vision) and your *how* (your values).

It is probable that when you first created these you may have done them on your own or maybe with an external advisor. If that were the case, my recommendation would be, this time around, to make this a more collaborative exercise and involve more stakeholders. This way you can ensure the revised version resonates with the different stakeholder groups, whose support you will need on the next phase of your business journey.

I refer to these three commitments as the organisational core. The strength of the core is key to optimal business performance. If everyone involved in your business understands your fundamental aims, and where they fit into these, they can support you and add their input. There is a lot of talk about 'Generation Z' (those born between the mid-1990s and early 2000s) being purpose driven and only wanting to work for organisations that are clear on their aims and making a difference to society. While this may be true, I don't think it is any different from previous generations. Ultimately we are talking about human needs and not generational needs. The needs we have fall into three categories: basic ones such as security and a wage; psychological ones, such as relationships and accomplishment; and finally self-fulfilment ones, such as achieving our ambitions and creative potential.

If you have a workforce that has not only their basic needs met but also both their psychological and self-fulfilment met by working for you, there is no doubt you will have a competitive advantage over those companies which have only focused on satisfying the basic needs of their workforce. For this to be a reality, you must be clear on your organisational core. Once you are clear, and communicate the core commitments, it is far easier to find other stakeholders who align with them, thus giving you a 'tribe', committed to making the journey with you.

Step 2: Being objective about the status quo
Where are you future proof, and where do you need to strengthen?

The most challenging of the steps is probably this. It requires you to visualise the future business you wish to create, and then detach yourself to consider what is required to do this. In this second step, you need to objectively assess what needs to change, what needs to grow, and what needs to be replaced entirely to make the transformation to the next level.

For instance, it may be that the person who has been dutifully running your finances for the past five years is not capable or suitable to oversee the future finances. In the same way, the financial software that was previously fit for purpose is now too basic, given the quality of information you now require.

The crucial outcome from this step is a future organisational chart showing the position you will need to fill and recruit for when the business has grown. It may be that some of your current employees can be trained and developed to take on bigger roles and more responsibility. But it is equally probable that you may need to recruit externally for specific skill sets you do not possess.

From your perspective as the leader, the crucial change needed is to create a senior leadership team below you that have the aptitude and appetite to run the business in the future. Only by doing this can you move from dependency to autonomy effectively. The team that assumes your role must have a greater sum of skills than you possess to effectively replace you. In simple terms, you need specialists that understand their specific function with greater depth than you do. This must happen if you are going to be freed of some of your current responsibilities.

You need to apply the same process to all areas of your business. Your systems, your processes, your brand, your offerings, etc. Keep asking yourself the same three questions:

➤ Is it future fit?

➤ Will it scale in alignment with the needs of the business?

➤ Does it still add value/relevance?

You need to give yourself permission to make the changes you require to create the company that you envisage in the future.

This is a tough step to take as you may feel a high degree of loyalty to your employees who have served you well thus far. However, this 'upgrading' of workforce, processes and systems is fundamental to achieving the transformation to maturity.

Step 3: Ensuring everyone is on board
Do you have buy-in across the organisation?

The final step is in theory the easiest, but for some leaders it can be quite daunting. Once you are clear on your redefined 'why, what and how' you need to effectively communicate this to your different stakeholders, so that they can buy in to the journey. This can be daunting as it may result in some objections and a raft of questions about where they fit into this. Both these responses should be encouraged, as any uncertainty or objections should be addressed as early in this process as possible. You need to be clear who is on board, and who is not. If you have created an aligned, inspiring set of core commitments, then the right employees (i.e. those who share your values and ambition) will be motivated.

At this stage of the process, you must remember and work in accordance with the guiding principles of alignment, transparency and vulnerability. In essence, the more aligned your thinking, the more transparent your reasoning can become, and the more vulnerable you can be in the way you present the information, the better. I will explain in more detail about the importance and impact of adopting these guiding principles in the next chapter.

An often-quoted example of an organisational buy-in to the core commitments concerns a meeting between John F. Kennedy and a janitor at NASA in the 1960s. When the president asked him what his role was, he answered, 'to put a man on the moon', echoing back the visionary pledge JFK had made.

Another example can be found back as far as the 17th century. Christopher Wren, one of the greatest of English architects, had been commissioned to build a new cathedral, St Paul's, in London. On one of his daily walks around the site, he asked three of the workmen individually the same question: 'What are you doing?' The first answered, 'I am cutting a piece of stone'; the second informed him that he was 'earning five shillings and two pence a day'; whereas the last man, unaware of Wren's identity, replied,

'I am helping Sir Christopher Wren build a beautiful cathedral.' The third workman understood the mission and vision in a way that the first two hadn't. He could see beyond the actual work, towards the bigger vision of creating a piece of art. Sharing your core commitments will enable you to convert workmen into cathedral builders!

Key takeaways
Summary

None of what I have encouraged you to think about and consider adopting in this chapter is a quick fix. Some of it might not be straightforward to understand and you may not agree with all of what I am proposing. It needs time, it needs resourcing, and it needs committed leaders to be a success. The prize is a big one: a company that operates with a high degree of autonomy that will allow you to have a healthier and more enjoyable relationship with your business.

As a leader, you have earned the luxury of choice in many areas of your life, but this can be a double-edged reward. In theory, it is always better to have choices rather than a single option, but there is also more riding on the outcome of your choices, now that you lead a larger company. The stakes are raised, so I would encourage you to objectively analyse to ensure you make the right choices for your business based on the challenges and changes you face.

Reflect and commit

Before moving on to the next chapter, I would encourage you to reflect on what the impact on yourself and your business would be if you were to embed the three ideologies proposed in these reflections.

1 Is now the right time to switch priorities and focus on becoming better before bigger?

2 Flucture: how can you add more structure and processes without curtailing the spontaneity and flexibility that has provided your success to date?

3 What would embracing the plateau look like for your business, and how could you increase the collaboration around a shared vision with all key stakeholders?

Now based on those reflections, what are you prepared to commit to change?

I will start...
I will stop...
I will do more...
I will do less...

What's next?
Foundational beliefs

In the next chapter we will focus on more specific behavioural changes that may need to take place across the leadership team to enable the transformation to occur smoothly, with maximum buy-in from the key stakeholders. Specifically, I will be introducing you to the guiding principles that sit around your core ideology.

3. Foundational Beliefs

Overview
A strong core
The importance of foundations

When you are building anything of any magnitude or ambition, creating stable, strong foundations is a worthwhile investment. Without these foundations you are unlikely to achieve the size or permanence you desire. A strong business needs secure psychological foundations comprising a number of elements, including your values, your mission, your vision and your beliefs. These elements may vary per business, but their presence in some form is necessary. The stronger and deeper these are, the easier you can construct your business around and on top of them.

These elements come from two equally important personal attributes: your ideology and your principles.

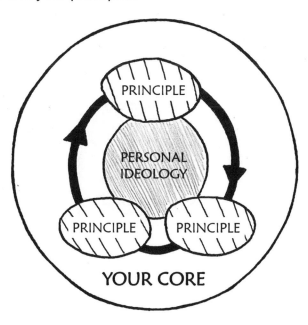

If you look at top performers in any walk of life, there are probably a number of characteristics or traits that contribute to their success. However, one trait common to all top performers is possessing a strong core. The term 'core' may refer to different aspects of their character and can be used in either a physical or mental sense. For instance, a top sportsperson will need to have a strong physical core in the muscles around the mid-section of their body, allowing them to maintain the optimal body position while they compete. Additionally, they will possess a belief in their ability to outperform their opponent (often referred to as mental toughness). Similarly, a top political leader will have a strong core belief system around which their policies and ideas are based.

There are two main benefits of having a strong core. First, it allows you to be consistent and reliable, which is a desirable trait in sport, politics or business. If a tennis player has a strong physical core, they will be able to achieve the optimal body position to hit their shots throughout a match. Whereas an opponent with lower core strength will start to lose the ability to maintain the optimal position much earlier in the match, and their performance will start to decline because of this weakness. A strong core is essential if you are going to achieve reliability. A political leader who has a strong core ideology will attract followers which this ideology resonates with; they will become ambassadors for that ideology. A political leader with a less defined ideology will find it difficult to get the same level of engagement, as their potential followers will be less certain of their aligning views.

In a business setting, stakeholders are attracted to businesses that are run by leaders with a strong and defined set of core mission, vision and values. This is because we have a human desire to support and connect with similar people, or those that we aspire to be like. Businesses that have a strong core are consistent and reliable, both of which are desirable traits for a consumer. This is how brands create a global presence, by delivering consumers the same brand experience irrespective of location or timing.

The second benefit of possessing a strong core is the confidence it can instil. A politician with a well-developed ideology has the confidence to debate in the open with political opponents, because they understand what points they want to communicate and how their view differs from their opponents. By making their concepts clear and tangible, they are likely to attract more followers and media attention, which in turn adds to their confidence. This has been demonstrated in a number of global elections, where an outside candidate, such as Trump, has outperformed expectations and rivals, partially due to the confidence and consistency of his messages and ideology. This confidence is based on a well-defined political ideology, i.e. a strong core.

This theory can be equally applied to a business setting. Here, the confidence demonstrated by leaders directly impacts on the perception of their company. This is particularly important when gaining the trust of their stakeholders. We want to root for and associate ourselves with confident leaders like Branson, Gates and Jobs, often irrespective of the quality of services they provide.

The power of 3

You will notice as you progress through this book that I often use sets of three. This is because I am a big believer in the power of three from marketing and learning perspectives. We can hold three concepts or ideas simultaneously; any more and we may start to forget detail, which is why marketers have been working to this principle for years.

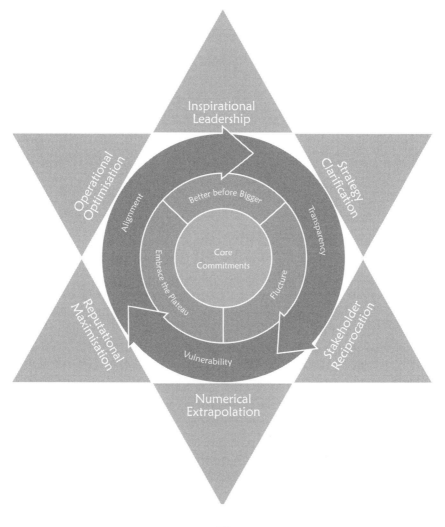

Guiding principles
A framework to operate from

My core ideology and guiding principles have evolved over 30 years via a combination of personal experience and first-hand observations of exceptional leaders. Like all frameworks they are both acquirable and constantly evolving; they should be continually challenged but importantly give you a starting point to work from. I would encourage you to adopt the framework I have articulated in the previous two chapters as your starting point. This will enable you to create momentum and focus, then over time you can explore whether there is a more appropriate version which is true for you.

Your ideology consists of your inner guiding principles that need to be complemented by outer manifestations. These two elements sit alongside each other like concentric circles.

In the previous chapter I have explained the three core elements of my ideology:

➤ *better before bigger*

➤ *flucture*

➤ *embrace the plateau.*

These constitute my inner beliefs both in a personal and business context.

Those beliefs are complemented by three guiding principles, which are their externally visible manifestations:

➤ alignment

➤ transparency

➤ vulnerability.

My personal experience, as the owner of two SMEs, has demonstrated how it is very difficult to scale a business without having these three guiding principles in place. With the wonderful value of hindsight I now realise that I did not have these three core principles in place, meaning my businesses were too reactive, too conservative and too random to be able to grow to their potential.

My coaching experience has allowed me to observe numerous business leaders closely to understand what makes them tick, and what holds them back. From these observations, it has become very clear to me how impactful the presence of a strong set of principles can be. Businesses run by leaders that embed their defined principles run more smoothly, grow more quickly, and can cope with more uncertainty.

My guiding principles

Principles as your primary colours

Red, yellow and blue are the three primary colours from which a multitude of other shades can be created. In this respect there is a strong analogy between primary colours and guiding principles. I see guiding principles as being the bases of multiple attributes, but if all three aren't present their impact is reduced.

When you combine two primary colours, a new colour is created; in the same way, when two guiding principles are present you generate a new attribute. I will explain how this works later in the chapter, but first let me introduce you to the guiding principles.

Principle 1: Alignment
Are you leading from the core?

This first principle is instrumental in pushing those with the desire to improve in the correct direction. Clarity on the purpose of activity is vital. Granted, it is important that time is focused on what you do and how you do it, but in great people, great teams and great organisations there is a compelling 'why' at the front and centre. This is their North Star and keeps them focused on moving closer to their vision.

During the early stages of organisational growth, it is necessary for leaders to spend most of their time focused merely on survival. Any leftover time can be focused on creating embryonic processes and internal roadmaps. The urgent priorities take precedent over the important ones. However, even during these more frenetic early years, enlightened business leaders will make sure that a business growth curve, setting out templates and manuals, is created. This will outline the 'what' and the 'how' with their own set of company values. This alignment will ensure others can operate the business and deliver the services accordingly. They appreciate the quickest way to achieve their 'why' is to keep it front and centre, whatever the circumstances or stage of business growth.

Better Before Bigger

A very good example of this type of leader is Ray Kroc who, in 1961, bought a small chain of fast food restaurants in Southern California, and over the next 23 years created the global phenomena that we know as McDonald's. When he died in 1983 the company was operating in 32 countries and had a turnover of £8 billion per annum. Kroc recognised from day one that to scale the business he needed a clear and detailed operations manual. He spent his time focusing just on this, as he knew once this was created, the business could scale exponentially. Kroc was very good on the 'what' and the 'how', but he kept his 'why' front and centre at all times, as is illustrated in this quote: 'If you work just for money, you'll never make it, but if you love what you're doing and you always put the customers first, success will be yours.'

The great things about reaching adulthood, in life or in business, is you have both a greater degree of freedom and the luxury of choice. You get to choose how you spend your most limited resource, your time, and where to focus your attention. As a business leader, it becomes imperative that you choose wisely if you want your business to reach its true potential. If you focus on making better widgets, or improving internal efficiency, when both are laudable uses of your time, you are only going to be making incremental improvements. By this stage in your business journey, you should have people around you that can do both tasks skilfully, who also have the time available to do them more diligently. In the spare time created, you can make the revolutionary change that your business needs to move through to maturity. If you feel your presence among the ground force is necessary, you haven't actually created an interdependent business; you have created a job for yourself instead!

Your objective should be to create a business that operates without your input, so that you can focus the majority of your time on your personal aims and company 'why'. Your business should be part of your life and not your whole life by this stage. Your business should serve you rather than the reverse being true.

If you think about your current relationship with your business which of the diagrams opposite best describes how you feel?

The key here is to make sure there is as much alignment and overlap between your personal 'why' and the company 'why' as possible. In Reality 1, the business dominates the relationship and your personal 'why' (your life) sits inside the business. This is a very limiting situation, as your personal growth is dependent on your business growth. This is where most businesses start off, as the relationship is hard-wired into our psyche as being the default of a successful entrepreneur. As the business grows, Reality 2 can be achieved with a healthier symbiotic relationship emerging between your business and your life. There is a degree of overlap, but you

Reality 1 – Your business being the dominant aspect of your life, which sits inside your business.

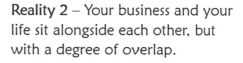

Reality 2 – Your business and your life sit alongside each other, but with a degree of overlap.

Reality 3 – Your business sitting inside your life.

have a life outside of your business. In an ideal situation we should all be inhabiting Reality 3, where there is no gap at all, and your company is actually an extension or manifestation of your personal 'why'. For instance, an entrepreneur passionate about organic food and the benefits it can bring who starts an organic food distribution business probably has a very similar personal and business 'why'. Their organic ideology is the greater, and the business is just a single manifestation of this.

If this has been achieved, then you can explore other manifestations of your 'why', with little risk that these other projects will negatively impact your core business. If you put the right team in place and have embedded the driving mentality into your company culture, you have given yourself the freedom to create further businesses with the same 'why'.

The structure you have created within the business now gives you the flexibility to explore other opportunities. If you keep your 'why' front and centre you are less likely to create dependency, and much more likely to achieve the personal satisfaction that is often missing during the adolescent phase of business growth.

There is a fitting quote from philosopher L.P. Jacks that sums up perfectly the first principle:

> A master in the art of living draws no sharp distinction between his work and his play; his labor and his leisure; his mind and his body; his education and his recreation. He hardly knows which is which. He simply pursues his vision of excellence through whatever he is doing, and leaves others to determine whether he is working or playing. To himself, he always appears to be doing both.
> – L.P. Jacks, *Education through Recreation* (1932), p. 1.

Principle 2: Transparency
Are you keeping the 'curtain up'?

By 'keeping the curtain up' we are forced to be honest, not just with others, but ourselves about what's working well and what needs to be improved. In doing this, we cease to delude or mislead ourselves.

In a business context, 'keeping the curtain up' means that we are open and clear with all stakeholders about how the company is performing against expectations. What's working better than expected and what areas need more work or improvement? The alternative is to work in secret, behind closed doors, keeping our numbers and strategies close to our chest, and only sharing them with a few trusted lieutenants. While this way of working is understandable, in some respects it demonstrates insecurity and a fear of failure. It also fails to encourage, or allow, any degree of engagement from the other stakeholders.

Running a business doesn't have to be, or shouldn't be, a solitary exercise. The leader should not shoulder the entire emotional and financial burden as the business scales. I spent too many years hiding behind the curtain I had erected – this meant that other stakeholders could not assist or shape the way the business operated. This was both tiring and ultimately costly, as the business didn't operate to its full potential, to the determinant of my stakeholders. The more enlightened leader realises this early in their business life cycle and creates an organisational support structure. This results in others being equally invested in the success of the business and sharing some of the emotional burden.

The Holy Grail is all employees adopting 'an employer's mentality', meaning they treat the business as if they owned it. This means they are considered in the decisions they make, they are conscious of how they spend their 'work' time, and they work in a proactive rather than reactive manner. For this Holy Grail state to be achieved, their leader must engage them first; this is achieved by 'keeping the curtain up'. From the employee's perspective this means they get to both see and understand how the business is performing. More importantly, they are encouraged to suggest solutions and improvements that will increase performance levels.

This principle may be a scary concept, but you can easily reframe it as liberating. It is illogical to believe that the leader of a growing business can possibly have all the solutions. As the business scales in both size and complexity, there are just too many challenges happening simultaneously for you to solve them all. At some stage, you need to empower others to find solutions, but this empowerment can't occur if you don't have transparency. Let them know all the factors involved, the timescales and the implications if you want them to devise the best answers in any given situation.

One of the major benefits of adopting and embedding transparency as one of your guiding principles is that it increases accountability. Accountability is that desirable situation when another party assumes responsibility to produce a pre-agreed outcome. You are a very interested observer/sponsor/cheerleader, but someone else carries the burden of expectation and the pressure to perform. Most businesses operate in a responsibility mode, which from my perspective is less effective.

One of the best examples of the accountability being generated by adopting transparency is in a weight loss group. Participants pay to be weighed in public, knowing this increases accountability, and makes them more likely to adhere to their agreed diet and exercise regime. They don't need to get weighed in public or join a group, but they know by 'keeping the curtain up' and by being transparent, they actually increase their chance of success. This also provides a support network to encourage them. In the same way, if business leaders are open with their employees and other stakeholders about their numbers and performance, they will not only receive their support and engagement, but also benefit from their suggested improvements.

The 'curtain up' principle is challenging for leaders to adopt, but once in place it enables you to be a more considered and liberated leader. You will be considered because you can choose when and where to take accountability. You will be liberated because the heavy burden of finding all the solutions will be released.

Principle 3: Vulnerability
Are you spending enough time outside your comfort zone?

My final guiding principle is vulnerability. This translates simply to regularly spending time outside your comfort zone. Progression and growth are rarely found by continuing along the same path.

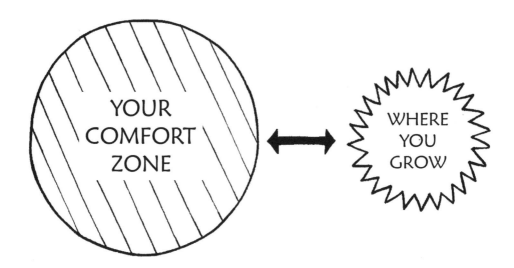

As author Michael Gerber observes in *The E-Myth Revisited*, 'Comfort makes cowards of us all.' We can easily let our comfort zones paralyse us, preventing us from acting against problems that are at once intimidating, but necessary to face. The desire to stay within the comfort zone increases the more time we spend in it; we start to convince ourselves that this is the 'only way' to operate, introducing the limiting beliefs, causing paralysis and procrastination (Chapter 2). We tell ourselves that things aren't as bad as we imagine, and that with just a few minor tweaks the outcome will be different. This is flawed thinking. We are convincing ourselves that evolution is required, when the reality is that revolutionary change is needed.

The flaw with this type of thinking was articulated very crisply by Albert Einstein who concluded, 'We cannot solve problems with the same thinking we used to create them.' Therefore, we need to step outside of the way we currently operate to see a different outcome or change some fundamental way in which the business currently runs. This is one of the critical skills that great leaders possess.

The reality of spending a higher proportion of time outside your current comfort zone, both as a leader and as a company, is that you may fail more. This is a difficult reality that you need to get comfortable with.

Leaders of successful mature businesses have the ability and foresight to see failures as a necessary part of the business growth cycle. The greatest take it one step further, rebranding 'failure' as a 'learning experience'. Now, on first read this may sound a little bit like HR mumbo jumbo, but on closer inspection there are some sound psychological and behavioural reasons why adopting this attitude really works. Linking back to my second principle, your employees and leadership are going to feel far more comfortable 'keeping the curtain up' if learning experiences are accepted as part of the organisational journey.

Why is this principle important? First, it will change the culture within your organisation. If employees feel secure in their agency to find alternative solutions, this will empower them to achieve more. They will start to develop a 'what if' mentality that all great inventors have. Conversely, if this mantra is not in place, your organisation may have a 'fear of failure' culture that is psychologically disabling, and can lead to procrastination at both the individual and organisational level. You, as leader, need to ensure this is not the case, not just in your words but in your actions. You must adopt this sentiment by Mark Twain:

Dance like no one is watching,
Live like you'll never be hurt
Sing like no one is listening
Live like it's heaven on earth.

Encourage your employees to adopt an 'owner's mentality' (principle 2 – transparency) where they are free to express themselves rather than fearing the consequences of their actions. This is vulnerability in action. Of course, I initially encourage you to add structure and process to your business, but once this is done, give employees the agency to find new solutions and challenge current operations. This attitude is often found in tech start-ups, full of creative people with lots of ideas and opinions, but it is less present in more established companies if structure and process are allowed to dominate.

There is a balance to be achieved, but if you find this, you will have an organisation that is simultaneously efficient and creative, which for most businesses is the ideal scenario.

As well as the psychological gains from this principle, there is also a related behavioural benefit to be had.

For most leaders of an adolescent business, there is a desire not to become the bottleneck through which all company decisions must be made. This total control was desirable and probably necessary during the start-up or infancy phase, when there were fewer defined operational processes in place and a trusting relationship with your employees had not yet been established. However, this way of operating soon becomes unsustainable as the business grows, and the number of decisions starts to multiply. The business leader soon becomes overwhelmed, and incorrectly feels the need to be part of every decision or operational discussion. The relationship they have inadvertently created with their employees is one of dependency. This relationship is counterproductive to growing the business and becoming a creative leader.

As a company moves from adolescence to maturity, one of the major benefits that should be felt by the leader is the freedom to return to their entrepreneurial roots. This can in turn create a culture that encourages entrepreneurial behaviour across the organisation, where learning experiences are embedded as part of the creative process. Employees can be encouraged and even rewarded to challenge the status quo, both within the organisation, and within the wider marketplace their company competes in.

Vulnerability is probably the most challenging of the three principles to adopt as it appears superficially to be counterintuitive. We are taught to avoid putting ourselves in situations where we don't have a high degree of control or are not sure of the outcome. However, to scale from adolescence to maturity that is exactly the behaviour that needs to be adopted at employee and business level across the company. Calculated risk-taking is necessary.

Desirable outcomes
Prioritising personal growth

Personal fulfilment is a continual journey of self-discovery and contentment with your position in life. It's about achieving the goals you most desire, rather than those set by culture or society. Your self-fulfilment is paramount. When we're our best selves, we can serve others with more desire, commitment and presence.

This may on first reading appear a selfish mindset, but if you think about when you've been most generous, and made your best contributions, it almost certainly when you are in a state of personal contentment. Having a clear personal ideology and a strong set of guiding principles is fundamental to achieving fulfilment. Both need to be embedded in the way you function before you can look to instil them into your organisation. Personal transformation always needs to precede organisational transformation.

While you will gain a degree of momentum and focus if you establish any one of the three fundamental principles, the real power is generated when at least two, and ideally all three, are present and in harmony. This can be drawn parallel to the analogy of these principles as primary colours, mixing to create new attributes. As the diagram below shows there are three attributes – clarity, confidence, and curiosity – that can be generated if you have all three principles present.

The three guiding principles

1 **Be aligned** – keep your WHY front and centre.

2 **Be transparent** – 'keep the curtain up'.

3 **Be vulnerable** – step outside your comfort zone.

The three desirable attributes

1 **Instilled curiosity** – become obsessed with known unknowns.

2 **Increased confidence** – become the leader your company needs.

3 **Improved clarity** – become crystal clear on who you are and who you're not.

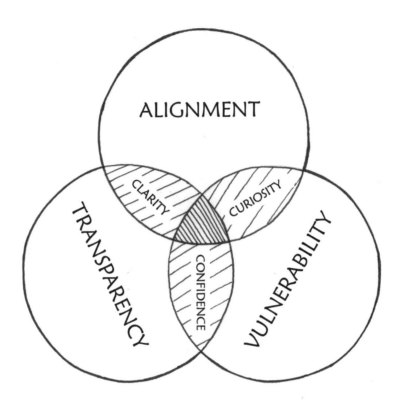

I believe fulfilment occurs when these three attributes are present simultaneously. Organisation fulfilment is more likely to happen when you're curious, confident and clear about who you are and where you're heading.

Mature companies display these attributes constantly. They are curious about what is next and where they can improve. They are confident to try new offerings, and attempt to create new markets. They are clear who their tribe is, and what their brand promise is.

In the same way that a writer needs to act like a professional author to finish and publish their first book, an adolescent business needs to think and act like a mature company to achieve their desired transformation. Let me explain in more depth how the presence of two principles creates a desirable attribute, and how this attribute will move you closer to fulfilment.

1. Instilled curiosity
Becoming obsessed with known unknowns

When alignment meets vulnerability

ALIGNMENT (VISION & VALUES)	ALIGNED	Boredom = SLOW PROGRESS	Instilled Curiosity = GROWTH
	MISALIGNED	Disengagement = STAGNATION	Fear = SLOW PROGRESS
		INSIDE	OUTSIDE
		VULNERABILITY (COMFORT ZONE)	

Former US Secretary of State, Donald Rumsfeld, once said this, as he responded to a question about the links between Iraq and weapons of mass destruction:

> Reports that say that something hasn't happened are always interesting to me, because as we know, there are known knowns; there are things we know we know. We also know there are known unknowns; that is to say, we know there are some things we do not know. But there are also unknown unknowns—the ones we don't know we don't know. And if one looks throughout the history of our country and other free countries, it is the latter category that tend to be the difficult ones.

Aside from the contextual minefield, this quote resonates with me because it summarises well the three options of focus that leaders have available to them on a daily basis.

➤ **Option 1** – focus on known knowns, things you already know and understand

➤ **Option 2** – focus on known unknowns, things that you should know but don't yet know

➤ **Option 3** – focus on unknown unknowns, things you don't yet know exist.

While option 1 may lead to some gradual improvements, the real value for me is to be had in options 2 and 3. A curious leader will spend the majority of their time exploring these options, as they know this will expand their knowledge, opening new avenues tactically and strategically.

Coming from a place of curiosity means you learn more and learn quicker. I appreciate it is relatively easier to focus on the known unknowns as you know what they are but harder to work on unknown unknowns, as they need to be discovered before you can work on them. To aid this discovery process it is crucial that leaders spend time with people outside of their normal circles, look into other industries and explore how things work outside of commercial operations, e.g. within the military.

As you can see from the 2x2 matrix above, only one of the four outcomes is positive – instilled curiosity leading to growth. In my experience, most adolescent business leaders are currently in a state of boredom or fear. If they are suffering from a sense of boredom, they have created a very 'safe' business, as they remain too far inside their own comfort zone. In the opposite corner, leaders demonstrating procrastination are suffering from a sense of fear. They probably have an exposed business, operating without fundamental values or vision. For either group a major shift in the way they operate is necessary to achieve the ideal state of instilled curiosity. Like any change programme, the first step is to correctly identify your current state, before you can progress and passionately embrace growth. You must create the necessary momentum to make the shift.

2. Increased confidence
Becoming the leader your organisation needs

When transparency meets vulnerability

TRANSPARENCY (OPENNESS)	CURTAIN UP	Frustration = SLOW PROGRESS	Increased Confidence = GROWTH
	CURTAIN DOWN	Apprehension = STAGNATION	Paranoia = SLOW PROGRESS
		INSIDE	OUTSIDE
		VULNERABILITY (COMFORT ZONE)	

The key element in defining the relationship between transparency and vulnerability is the level of confidence exhibited by leaders. If both principles are in place, confidence will be high, but if either is missing, slower progress towards the vision is likely. If a business operates with a 'curtain down' mentality, growth is likely to be less than optimal, resulting in (mild) paranoia. This is because the leader may be operating outside their comfort zone but hasn't made other stakeholders aware of this, so lacks their support. The way to break this state is to focus on becoming more transparent. Invite stakeholders 'behind the curtain' and explain what is happening. Let them know the aims and give them the opportunity to contribute to the process where appropriate.

On the opposite side of the matrix, transparency is present, but vulnerability is not; this will lead to a sense of frustration. If this is the case, maybe start with one department of the company, or one specific team, and encourage them to name the frustrations they feel so you can start to work collaboratively on the solution. Let them know why you are feeling frustrated, as they are probably already aware (unless you have a great poker face), but they may not realise the root cause. You need to demonstrate the behaviour you want to see in them; let them be vulnerable too. Tell them you've got their backs if they fail when trying something new.

The quicker (and perhaps scarier) option is to inject a larger dose of transparency simultaneously to spending time outside the organisational comfort zone. I am not necessarily advocating introducing these measures company-wide from the offset. In the same way a stand-up comedian may try out new material with a smaller selected audience before adding it to their main act. Digital companies regularly use this approach when they offer a beta version of a new product to a selected audience. This approach allows them to stay both lean and agile, as they are not over-investing until they receive positive feedback. If the feedback is good, this will give you the organisational confidence to invest more resources into this service or product line.

3. Improved clarity
Become crystal clear on who you are and who you're not
When transparency meets alignment

TRANSPARENCY (OPENNESS)	CURTAIN UP	Confusion = SLOW PROGRESS	Improved Clarity = GROWTH
	CURTAIN DOWN	Uncertainty = STAGNATION	Disengagement = SLOW PROGRESS
		MISALIGNED	ALIGNED
		ALIGNMENT (VISION & VALUES)	

In much the same way as confidence is the key element in the previous scenario, the relationship between alignment and transparency is dictated by the degree of clarity within a company. If there is no clarity about elements such as vision, company values, core competencies and key differentiators, it is very unlikely that optimal growth will be achieved. Organisations that lack clarity tend to suffer from slow progress or confusion, as everyone pulls in different directions. The lack of clarity impacts key stakeholder groups, as they remain unclear on the company's mission and their role within this. In contrast, a company with organisational clarity throughout presents a positive message to each stakeholder group about their expectations. In return the leader gets a high level of engagement and lots of feedback, enabling the business to continually improve and iterate its offering.

If you are clear on your core commitments such as your mission, your vision and your values, but have not effectively articulated those to the stakeholders, you will probably feel disengaged. If the audience doesn't understand it's not their fault; it's the leader's job to communicate effectively.

In the adjacent corner of the matrix, a sense of confusion exists if you act without alignment to your core commitments, being too random with the way the company is led. Impulsive leadership can result in damaging decisions being made without sufficient consideration. To remove confusion you must increase alignment and demonstrate the link between the decisions you make and the progress towards the aspirational vision.

Lack of clarity can be a by-product of rapid growth and, if unresolved, will slow the rate of future progress. Therefore, the presence of both alignment and transparency are key to keep leaders accountable to their own vision and their stakeholders.

Key takeaways
Summary

After working alongside business leaders for the past 30 years, I have observed some very great, some average and some less good leadership styles. Interestingly, the great leaders tended to operate from a similar set of principles. They were consistent in action, which made it easier for those around them to operate. Their leadership is predictable but, in a reassuring not uninspiring way. When principle-based leadership is in place then trust levels are high, and when trust is high, performance follows.

Reflect and commit

Before moving on to the next chapter, I would encourage you to reflect on what the impact on yourself and your business would be if you were to operate in conjunction with the guiding principles outlined.

1 Is the way you lead your company aligned with your core commitments (your vision, mission and values)?

2 Are you being transparent enough with your various stakeholders to enable them to assist you in achieving your vision?

3 Do you spend enough time outside of your comfort zone in a vulnerable space?

Now based on those reflections, what are you prepared to commit to change?

I will start ...
I will stop ...
I will do more ...
I will do less ...

What's next?
Critical component #1: *Inspirational leadership*

Having a clear ideology and operating with a set of guiding principles are the first two factors required to start the transformation from adolescence to maturity. However, these alone won't necessarily create the mature, self-operating organisation you desire. For that to materialise, there are six critical components, which must be embedded in your operations. The first of these is *inspirational leadership*.

4. Inspirational Leadership

Overview

Why is *inspirational leadership* a core component?

Are you setting the standards high enough?

Without wanting to state the obvious, the quality of leadership across any organisation is arguably more influential than any other component, in relation to performance. The way a company is led determines how it is perceived by its various stakeholders, and how sustainable and profitable it is. It is very unlikely that a respected, long-standing and viable company does not have quality leadership at its core.

The impact that the quality of leadership has also increases as the company scales. A small start-up can get by with a great product or great service, but as more stakeholders are added and the complexity of the business increases, leadership becomes more important. If the quality of leadership within a business does not increase with a sharper trajectory than the overall growth, progression may stagnate. Leadership capability needs to be treated in the same way as any other skill set in the business: it should be continually assessed and invested in.

As well as increased complexity as the business grows, the style of leadership also needs to develop in alignment with this growth. A style that works successfully in a small start-up operation does not necessarily work as effectively in a larger concern. This is a difficult truth for some leaders to accept, as it puts the onus on them to be continually developing and adapting their leadership style. I will explain later in the chapter about the changes and adaptations I believe leaders need to make.

Inspirational leadership does not apply only to those at the top of the organisational chart, but to anyone within the company who has a leadership responsibility. As a company grows more leaders need to appear across all levels of the company if the successful transition to maturity is going to be made.

How adolescents normally approach leadership
The current problem

My experience has been that leaders can often default back into spending too much time in the lesser role of being a functional manager, and thereby not spending enough time as the inspirational leader required.

In many ways a functional manager is the polar opposite of an inspirational leader:

➤ The manager generally operates in a reactive mode while the leader prefers to work proactively.

➤ The manager focuses on achieving optimal efficacy out of company resources, as opposed to the leader who is concerned primarily with effectiveness.

➤ The manager is hands on in their approach and functions as part of the team, whereas a leader operates with more perspective and with a gap between their focus and teams.

➤ The manager implements the strategy devised by the leader.

Functional managers are common and can be found in most companies. Inspirational leaders are rare, which partly explains why so few companies successfully transition from adolescence to maturity.

I'm not suggesting that functional managers are not required, but if there are only functional managers at the heart of a business (or leaders with a functional manager mindset), the chances of that business realising its potential are greatly reduced. This is mainly because there is no one stretching the organisation's horizons and ability in the way an inspirational leader naturally does. As Einstein observed, it is very difficult to solve a problem or challenge with the same level of thinking that created the problem in the first place.

A very small proportion of infant and adolescent businesses make it to maturity; I strongly believe that a lack of inspirational leadership is the single most important factor underpinning that reality.

Whether we are talking about the general public or employees in a business, neither group want to be managed. Individuals generally don't reach their full potential when they are being controlled. Employees want to be led; they respond to the actions and words of those they admire. Leaders who challenge them to take responsibility and action to be the best version of themselves. Leadership should be based around the principles of engagement and empowerment, which encourage people to improve.

Functions, processes and systems can be managed efficiently, but individuals and organisations need to be led effectively to reach their full potential. However, leadership alone is not enough, as the role can just be inherited or assigned to someone in which case it can be very passive. What is required here is *inspirational leadership*, which is conscious but all too rare.

How mature companies are led
The ideal scenario

If we accept the premise that one of the main differences between an adolescent and mature company is the amount and quality of leadership present, it is essential that we dive deeper into what constitutes 'quality' leadership. For me, 'quality' can be defined by the presence of inspiration.

Inspiration can be broken down to three key ingredients: ingenuity, intention and intensity:

Ingenuity is defined as the ability to be clever, original or inventive in the way you act. In leadership terms, this would be apparent in a business strategy or the solution to an organisational challenge. Ingenuity can be characterised as thinking outside the box, or the ability to identify an alternative solution. It is a dormant quality for most of us that only appears if we create the appropriate environment. The main ingredient required here is time. All too often we react hastily to a situation rather than give ourselves the time to craft a considered response. *Inspirational leadership* understands the difference between quickly but inaccurately reacting, and responding in a measured way – and by preference will always choose the latter.

There needs to be an **intention**, a plan or a vision at the centre of what is being proposed. If there is no clear outcome, then you are unlikely to inspire others. To be a true leader you need followers, and followers need to have something to aspire to. The articulation of this aspiration is the catalyst for others sharing it to follow and support them. No aspiration, no intention. The intention in a business setting is most often conveyed via the mission statement or company vision. This is where the leader has the opportunity to present the purpose of the business, i.e. their purpose, and their desired destination. If the purpose and/or destination resonate with stakeholders, the leader will have created momentum aligned to their intention. The intention is the 'why' binding the stakeholders together, and the fuel needed to sustain the journey. The clearer and more alluring the intention, the larger and more fanatical the tribe of followers generated. Inspirational leaders know that a clearly stated, unambiguous intention is key to generating a following to support them on their mission.

The final element is **intensity**. It is not enough to be clever and to have a plan, you also need to be passionate and single minded about achieving it. Intensity is the energy that you bring to a situation, and it is contagious. Simply, people need to know that you care about the intention. There is nothing more uninspiring than a leader presenting a vision in a detached manner, as if they were a newsreader reading an auto-prompt. Fanatical followers will only be generated if they can see, feel or hear your passion. Inspirational leaders appreciate that their passion towards the intention is critical.

If all three of these elements can be aligned and amalgamated, then inspiration will exist. Without these, a leader will have to rely more heavily on perspiration than inspiration. Perspiration is limited; inspiration can be infinite.

Functional managers work hard; inspirational leaders work smart. Adolescent companies work hard; mature companies work both hard and smart.

Considerations

Before explaining the three essential elements that underpin *inspirational leadership*, I want to highlight a few factors that may influence your current leadership style.

Nature or nurture?
How do we improve the quality of leadership?

There have been many articles written on whether great leaders are born, or leadership skills are learned from experience. I believe it's a combination of both. Some people are natural leaders, and others have leadership forced upon them. In my coaching career I have come across many people who by their admission weren't natural leaders who had to adopt a prominent role because they were either the business founder or best technician available. However, through a combination of personal development and experience they have become real, effective leaders. Great leaders can definitely be developed, rather than recruited. If the right environment exists, and the required investments are made, there is no reason why future leaders can't be created from within. Often it is far harder to integrate a new leader into your existing company culture than it is to develop high-performing employees. These employees already understand the company culture and vision to a depth that would be hard to instil in an external hire.

Leadership can be improved, like most aspects of a business. You need the humility and self-awareness to accept that as a leader you're a work in progress, having the vulnerability to ask where you can improve. It's up to others to judge how inspirational you are. Without demonstrating the humility to ask, how are you going to know how to improve?

While I am a strong advocate for developing leadership within a company, I accept that sometimes it will be necessary to recruit a more experienced or proven leader to strengthen your team. This can work well if you have clarity on the type of leader needed, a rigorous recruitment system to filter out unsuitable candidates, and an effective integration process to bed them in.

The key here is recognising that for most leaders the real learning starts on the job, whether this is developing leaders from within or recruiting externally.

Achieving a balanced perspective

Are you applying the Switzerland principle?

One of the biggest challenges for a novice leader is to achieve neutrality. This means finding a balanced perspective between the competing interests and demands of the various stakeholder groups.

A novice leader, uncertain of their ability, will often be swayed or unduly influenced by the most vociferous stakeholder group. Some leaders will operate a very customer-centric business which may disregard the needs of other stakeholder groups. Other leaders will be very team-centric, stating that their people are the most important element within their business, prioritising their demands. The third type of leader focuses more on the needs of the shareholders (including themselves in many circumstances), creating a business which works almost exclusively towards maximising profits. While each may be positively received by the specific stakeholder group, favouring one will have negative consequences on the overall business.

A customer-centric organisation can suffer from high staff turnover and low profitability, as customer satisfaction is placed ahead of staff interests and shareholder returns. If the majority of profits are reinvested in new ways to keep customers happy that can give a short-term win but is unsustainable. Adolescent stage companies need to keep their staff and shareholders on board during the challenging growth phase by making sure reinvestment in improving the skills and reward packages for employees and paying dividends to shareholders.

An employee-centric company, while probably having very few challenges in finding and retaining great team members, will probably be churning through its customer base quickly. Consequently, increased customer acquisition costs will be required. This will also lead to lower profitability. Adolescent companies need a strong and loyal customer base to grow from, as much as they need a core team of loyal employees.

A shareholder-centric company will suffer from low engagement levels both amongst its employees and customers. As any profit being made is taken out of the business by the shareholders, rather than reinvested. These businesses will have a continual challenge to find new employees and new customers as the churn rate for both will be high. The extra cost of finding these groups will have a negative impact on profitability, resulting in lower future returns for investors. This demonstrates short-term thinking.

So, if none of these positions is either sustainable or desirable, what is the solution you may ask? The solution is to base your leadership approach around something that unites the three key stakeholders: your company values.

The values are a set of beliefs that underpin and dictate how the business should act and operate.

By focusing on values rather than needs, you put the interest of the business ahead of the interests of any single stakeholder group. Leadership should not be about gaining short-term adulation; it should be about earning long-term respect, which can only be achieved from a neutral and objective standpoint.

Finding your style
How far have you evolved?

Effective leaders have one fundamental element in common: they are comfortable in their own skin. By this I mean they have found a style of leadership that works both for them, but more crucially for those they lead. It's not about being a preset type of leader, as often your leadership may have to adapt depending on the situations face. If you become too predictable in the way you lead, this can work against you, but you should continue to act consistently with your underlying beliefs and values. Your stakeholders need to know what you stand for and what to expect from you.

When it comes to leadership, predictability is generally regarded as positive rather than negative; society recognises and admires strong leaders with a definitive point of view. We admire a leader for their passion and ability to articulate their views, without necessarily agreeing with their sentiment. However, as we mature, our leadership style will evolve, as we get more confident and comfortable in our role. During business infancy, new leaders will try out different styles, seeking approval from those around them. In adolescence, leaders are likely to experiment with new styles until they find one that fits best, becoming comfortable and confident. They will look to spend time with those who share and affirm their views. At some point during this maturing phase, they gain the wisdom and confidence to bring people into their inner circle who see the world differently and may challenge their perspectives. This is a clear sign of a mature individual, when they choose to consider contrasting points of view as a way of learning.

The one aspect that should remain constant during growth is our commitment to our core ideology and beliefs. These form the bedrock which *inspirational leadership* is built on. These are the immoveable pillars that bring strength, certainty and confidence to both ourselves and those we lead.

Before implementing the essential elements outlined in the rest of this chapter, it is worth reflecting on whether any of these considerations are negatively impacting the way your company is currently being led. If this is the case, what do you need to put in place to nullify their impact?

Essential elements & desirable attributes

1. Audacious visualisation
If you can't see the future clearly, how can you lead people there?

Being able to visualise the future is probably the essential element that all leaders need to have. If a leader demonstrates uncertainty in either the direction of travel, or belief in the vision, this has a negative impact on the morale and commitment of those they lead.

A good example of a leader demonstrating the power of visualisation can be found in John F. Kennedy's speech in 1961, when the president stated: 'I believe that this nation should commit itself to achieving the goal, before this decade is out, of landing a man on the moon and returning him safely to the earth.'

What resonates most with me is how specific the commitment was, enabling a whole nation to see the vision he was painting. Just eight years later, the vision was realised, and something which had seemed improbable was achieved, demonstrating the power of visualisation. Inspirational leaders must be audacious, possessing more than the normal amount of visualisation. The bigger the vision, the more inspiring it generally is to those you are looking to engage.

The thing to remember here is what may seem audacious to them (your stakeholders) may not feel audacious to you. Leaders generally have a higher degree of optimism, and a greater confidence in their own abilities than those they lead. Audacity is both relative and contextual.

> Shoot for the moon… even if you miss, you'll land among the stars. It's better to aim high and miss, rather than to aim low and hit. Get a bigger dream!
> – Les Brown

Before I talk about the specific attributes that underpin visualisation, I need to clarify the difference between a vision and a dream. A vision, while far reaching and seemingly difficult to achieve, is reality based. There is a practicality to a vision that is not necessarily present in a dream. Dreams are random, fleeting and often unattainable; visions are constant and consistent in their nature.

To achieve the required level of audacious visualisation there are three specific attributes you need to possess, these are:

i. storytelling

ii. duality

iii. personalisation.

i. Storytelling
Can you engage your audience?

It's not enough to be able to see the future clearly to be an inspirational leader, you need to be able to communicate that vision in a way that engages those you lead. Storytelling is one of the oldest professions; before the written word, verbal storytelling was the only way to communicate. Those who told the best stories gained authority, because they were trusted, and their stories were accepted, becoming reality.

Whether you are looking to engage a group of pre-schoolers, a gang of youths or your employees, your ability to bring your vision to life is crucial in gaining their attention and the respect of the group. Facts and numbers may be needed to back up the story, but without an engaging narrative the specificities are uninteresting.

With the range of communication channels open today, telling stories is easier than ever before. As demonstrated by the YouTube phenomenon, the younger generation intrinsically knows that it is as much about the quality of the story as it is about the knowledge you present. It's all about the 'show'.

To inspire someone to make a change, to take action, to make an investment, you need to convince them the reward will be worth it. Being a good storyteller is one of the attributes all 21st-century leaders need to possess.

ii. Duality
Are you equally comfortable in both the present and the future?

The second attribute counterbalances the first in some respects, being the ability to operate in both the present and the future. While storytelling is desirable, a consideration of the current situation is essential. Being able to operate comfortably between the two, sometimes contrasting states is an acquirable skill for most of us. We need to simultaneously deal with the present, but not lose sight of the bigger vision. This is where the quality of the team around you comes in to play. At some stage in your business growth, you need to be comfortable handing over the day-to-day operations to a team of trusted lieutenants, leaving you the space to focus more on the future than the present.

In an infant business most of our focus is on the here and now, as we are in survival mode. As the company grows, this tends to stay the main focus, as we have more operational level challenges to solve. However, what companies need to be doing at this stage is spending more time on planning for the future, otherwise they will never escape the present. There will always be operational-level problems that divert resources and time away from this. Inspirational leaders realise that even if their employee's solutions don't match their own style, this is necessary for them to switch focus. If everyone in the organisation is focusing fully on the here and now, who is doing the research and development, who is looking at market trends, etc.?

The inspirational leader possesses enough duality to support current operational aspects but spends the majority of their time on future planning. It is a tough balancing act to achieve but a necessary one. You need to be comfortable switching between the opposing states as required, which is an acquired attribute.

iii. Personalisation (WIIFM)
Are you able to make it personal?

WIIFM (What's In It For Me?) is apparently the mantra for the millennial generation. There is greater opportunity for them than any previous generation, which means they can be more selective with their time, attention and contribution. Millennials are going to make up an ever-increasing proportion of the workforce, so a key attribute for any leader is the ability to make a vision, a situation or an opportunity about them and not about you.

On first consideration this may come across as a selfish or self-serving stance, but when you dig a little deeper it comes down to a more rounded and objective understanding. We only have a certain amount of time to allocate to work and given millennials have much more choice than their predecessors, they are more considered about who they commit their working hours to. They're picky about who they choose to engage with, either as employee, contractor or customer. Their WIIFM attitude seems to demonstrate a healthier consideration than previous generations about where work should fit into their priorities. Therefore, as leader, you need to make sure it is crystal clear what the benefit of working for your company is. Most people will play games for the glory of winning, for the trophy, or for the recognition, so while financial rewards are important, they are not the only motivating factor, or even arguably the most effective one.

Instinctively, an inspirational leader understands their followers well enough to position what they are 'selling' in a way that appeals to them. They make it personal.

A key attribute of visualisation is understanding what's in it for *them* and not just you. If you can bring meaning to the vision, then they will follow.

Visualisation is a skill that can be learned and developed. The challenge for most leaders is that they don't give themselves the time and space to work on this role. They are more comfortable doing rather than thinking, underplaying the power that a well-articulated vision can have.

2. Pathos persuasion
Can you get them to see what you see?

History often portrays great leaders as strong alpha males, or Amazon-like women, who lead through the strength of their words and deeds. They are portrayed as having no obvious weaknesses and are single minded in their approach.

The reality of leadership in the 21st century is very different. It's about persuasion as much as rhetoric, and about collaboration rather than coercion. Being able to persuade others, and being open to persuasion by weight of evidence, are essential elements that a modern leader must possess. There are numerous ways you can persuade others that they should follow you, or implement your requests, but by far the most effective is *pathos persuasion*. In this context, *pathos* means convincing people with an argument that is designed to prompt an emotional response. In simple terms, they need to feel some of what you feel. You need to appeal to their emotions, not just their logic.

In some respect the first element of *audacious visualisation* is easier to achieve. The bigger the vision, the greater challenge you set for yourself as a persuader. It is a difficult balance to achieve, to set the bar high enough to inspire action, but low enough to feel achievable. If JFK had set the vision to put a man on Mars, what do you think would have happened? The chances are that after a few months/years of trying, NASA would have realised that it didn't have the capability, knowhow or resources to achieve this, and would have lost motivation and belief. Passion can only carry people so far, but it's the firelighter you need when you are introducing a new idea, concept or mission.

There are three desirable attributes that underpin this element of *inspirational leadership*:

i.   trust

ii. active listening

iii. open to change.

i. Trust
Do they believe in you, and vice versa?

For leaders of adolescent stage businesses, trust becomes one of the most crucial issues to embrace. To grow further, you need to start trusting others to take on some of the operational level decisions that you previously took alone. If the business is going to achieve its full potential, you must place more trust in those around you, more independent of your personal input. You must believe in the processes, the people and the plans you have put in place. Be the change you want to see in others. If you can demonstrate to others that you trust them, you will automatically gain loyalty.

At this stage in your business growth cycle it is imperative you surround yourself with people who have confidence in you to do the right thing at the right time. If they don't, you have either recruited poorly (hired people unaligned with your values), or not trained them well enough.

Newton's third law of motion simply states 'for every action, there is an equal and opposite reaction'. If you have chosen well, and trained appropriately, why wouldn't you trust them?

Trust equals freedom. If you have a team you trust (and who trust you) then you are free to be the leader your company needs. If you don't believe in others you will be held back by fear, which will negatively impact your personal growth, and the growth trajectory of the business. A lack of trust means that you will spend too much time either micromanaging others, or double-checking their work, neither of which is a productive use of your time. Importantly, both micromanaging and persistently checking will also negatively impact the performance of those reporting to you, knocking their confidence.

Trust can be easily lost, but also easily gained if you have the skills to do so and acknowledge its importance. The formula that underpins gaining trust is very simple: tell people the outcome you would like to see, ask them what assistance/clarification they need from you, then let them get on with the task. It's that simple; clarify, support, and detach. The more you implement this, the easier it becomes until it is established as one of your default attributes. Yes, there may be some bumps along the way, but it will serve you far better in the medium term than attempting to stay in control of every situation.

ii. Active listening
Were you listening, or did you just hear them?

There is a subtle, yet sizeable difference between hearing and listening. One is passive and one is active. We can hear the music, but do we listen to the lyrics? One creates pleasure; the other creates a reaction. *Active listening* is a two-way process where the recipient has understood not just the words spoken, but also the meaning and sentiment behind them.

It's essential that leaders listen to what others say about them, about their strategy, and about their brand. Nothing takes place in a vacuum, and our actions have consequences both on personal and wider societal levels; therefore, it's essential that we take the time to listen and understand the consequences.

Leadership is about accountability and owning the outcomes of your actions. *Active listening* ensures that before you try to persuade someone else of your point of view, you have fully understood theirs. As Stephen Covey states in *The 7 Habits of Highly Effective People: Powerful Lessons in Personal Change*:

> If I were to summarise in one sentence the single most important principle I have learned in the field of interpersonal relations, it would be this: Seek first to understand, then to be understood.

The key to mastering active, rather than passive, listening is having the ability (and confidence) to feed back immediately on what you've been told, so you can understand the details and sentiment thoroughly. By initially spending time clarifying, you demonstrate your active involvement in the process, and more importantly you show your desire to correctly understand what's been articulated. By doing this, you send a subliminal message that their words are inherently important. If this is done effectively and often it increases trust between the two parties and encourages the 'junior' partner to express an opinion more often. If we know that we're genuinely involved in a two-way dialogue, rather than a pseudo-listening exercise, we become more invested. Therefore, we will potentially offer deeper insights than we might have previously.

To do this effectively you need to focus more attention on the specific detail of what is said, and the intonation this is delivered with. This means you can effectively pick up both the meaning and the feeling behind the words. Too many people spend time planning their response when the other person is speaking, missing what is actually being said.

Most leaders are used to being the prominent speaker in meetings, but effective leaders realise it is better to speak last, allowing more time for *active listening*. You already know the information you intend to impart, so take the opportunity to listen first and understand other points of view. Inspirational leaders have the confidence to encourage alternative viewpoints or consider different strategies. They appreciate the simple process of listening to someone else creates trust and opens new opportunities.

Leaders who make listening to others' points a priority are rare, and those that regularly demonstrate *active listening* are even rarer. Saying this, inspirational leaders are also rare, and I am confident that those two facts are linked.

iii. Open to change
Are you sure about that?

Being persuadable can often be associated with weakness and indecision; however, the root of many problems can be traced back to a blinkered attitude. There is a difference between strong leadership and arrogant leadership. A strong leader is willing to admit that sometimes they need to alter their position, either because circumstances have changed, or new information has become available. This is the logical way to operate.

Stubbornness is neither desirable nor attractive in a leader, whereas listening and reacting to people's views is engaging and builds trust. By being persuadable you demonstrate that you're not shackled by your previous position. An obvious example of this is U-turning. A less confident leader would probably see a U-turn as a sign of weakness, and therefore stick to their previous point of view, irrespective of any changes in circumstance or opposing evidence. In contrast, a confident leader possesses the self-awareness to know that altering their position in light of new information is sometimes the best strategy. They can admit that their point of view has changed because of new data or evidence. This demonstrates humility, and also frees them from the constraints of a previous belief that they may feel duty bound to adhere to.

Rather than perceiving weakness, I admire leaders that demonstrate their willingness to reconsider if new facts become apparent or circumstances alter. I see these leaders as more in tune, more aware and less concerned with appearing omniscient. They appreciate that selecting the right option is more important than being limited by previous decisions.

As a follower I wouldn't expect my leader to be right all the time, which would be illogical and unrealistic. What we look for in leaders is confidence, not arrogance. We value honesty and transparency and will follow people who deliver on those attributes.

3. Visible empowerment
The freedom gained by sharing the spotlight

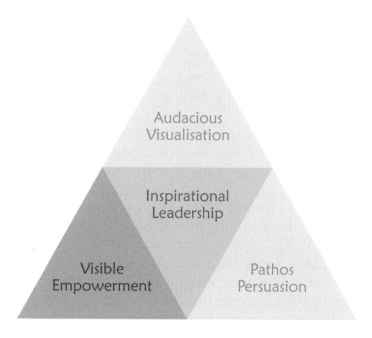

The third essential element that must be present in *inspirational leadership* is a sharing of responsibility, which I characterise as *visible empowerment*. 'Empowerment' has been an overused word in business for a while now and may have lost some of its importance because of this overuse; however, I still see it as a non-negotiable for ambitious organisations. I don't see how a business can become an interdependent, autonomous company without empowerment to free its leaders, allowing them more time on future-gazing. Without this, and more specifically *visible empowerment*, then companies will remain too leader dependent to scale successfully. Empowerment can lack some impact if it's not visible, or overt in manner; this can be achieved through transparency.

There is a powerful scene in the historical drama *The Last Kingdom*, when *visible empowerment* takes place as the ailing King Alfred deliberately waits for his son (and soon to be successor) to order their troops to engage the enemy. Although their advantage is being lost whilst the king waits for his son to summon the required courage, Alfred knows this is part of the process of empowerment and therefore a price worth paying.

For *visible empowerment* to take place and become embedded there are three specific attributes leaders need to possess:

i.   walking your talk

ii. having a compass but not the map

iii. consulting early and wide.

i. Walking your talk
Just show me, don't keep telling me!

Walking the talk is about going first and showing others the way. Sometimes this may mean stepping outside of your comfort zone. It is about being authentic; it simply means you fulfil your promises, and do not shy away from tough decisions. Your followers will accept a little hardship along the journey and will put in the extra hours, as long as they know their leaders are doing the same. Honesty is paramount here, and the more comfortable you can get with having a transparent organisation the better.

Employees expect to see their leaders mixing with them for at least some of the time, not hidden away in metaphorical glass towers and endless meetings. Walking your talk means making yourself available to discuss your vision when your followers need you to. It also means being transparent about how well you are progressing. Celebrate milestones with the team as they are achieved, but also admit when the business is off course or underperforming.

This is an attribute that relies on implementing the guiding principles of alignment, transparency and vulnerability. By practising these you are more likely to lead others to replicate your behaviour.

ii. Having a compass but not the map
Over to you, team...

Devolving some power goes against the basic human need of certainty, but it's a very important attribute to possess when you are encouraging others to take on more responsibility. By handing over some of the decision-making powers (an element of certainty) and letting others choose the most appropriate route (via the map), you send a clear message of trust. This constitutes a very visible transfer of responsibility. You supply the map but offer others the opportunity to lead using it. Of course, your input will sometimes still be required, but if you step in too early, you will undermine the trust you've established. If you step in too late, when things are not heading positively towards your goal, you may not achieve your desired outcome; it's a tough balance to find.

A wise leader will appreciate that any failure that may occur is at least partly their responsibility as they chose the person to empower, and they are ultimately answerable for how well they were trained and briefed. Failure and underperformance in 'junior' leaders and managers are down to the organisation more than the individual. Sharing responsibility and then standing back to observe is one of the most effective ways of measuring how well your organisation can develop suitable future leaders.

For employees (who are potential leaders) and partners there are two factors whose presence will enhance this desired movement towards greater empowerment. First, if there is a 'no-blame' mentality ingrained in the organisation's culture then you give the individuals concerned a greater probability of succeeding, they don't have to be so worried about potential failure. Second, there needs to be a detached, but experienced, leader in the background overseeing the mission, without being too deeply involved, only intervening if it is necessary. The presence of this leader will give an additional layer of security, which again will give first-time leaders the freedom from concern that may otherwise hamper their performance. The more senior leader is the co-pilot who only steps in if the mission is going considerably off course or, in their view, is unlikely to achieve the target destination within the pre-agreed timeline. As with a compass – here the budget, strategic plan and/or performance metrics – make sure the direction of travel is broadly correct.

iii. Consult early and consult wide
So who is with me?

The final attribute of an empowering leader is that they have both the ability and confidence to consult with other parties early in the planning process. They appreciate that to gain the trust of their colleagues/ employees, they must feel involved in the process with the opportunity to feed back.

From the leader's perspective, although painful to hear, it's far better to have any gaps or miscalculations pointed out early, so they can be corrected before any real damage is done. Internal and external focus groups are a great way to achieve this and can give you instant feedback on what you propose.

A confident leader is happy to test their strategy because positive feedback is reassuring, and negative feedback is constructive. Both outcomes are beneficial.

This also alludes to one of the qualities that inspirational leaders need to possess – humility. Counterintuitively admitting you don't know something can build confidence in your leadership rather than reducing it. Humility is seen as a positive trait and one we admire in our leaders. An inspirational leader knows that getting the best plan is more important than being seen as the fount of all knowledge.

Effective implementation doesn't mean always leading from the front. Yes, some of the time you need to be the strident leader, but other times, it is better to allow space for others to lead and contribute. Your role changes, and facilitation becomes the key skill you need to demonstrate to ensure the overall plan is implemented effectively. Experienced leaders know that working *with* their team is far more productive than working *through* their team; that is why *visible empowerment* is an essential element in a leader's toolbox. Inspirational leaders know and demonstrate that outcomes are all important; the more they empower their team, the more likely these outcomes will be desirable.

Case study

Ernest Shackleton

You know you are an inspiring leader when you can place a job advert that includes the words 'certain return doubtful', and you end up with a queue of applicants around the block. This was apparently the case when Ernest Shackleton placed an advert to recruit men for his second expedition to the Antarctic in 1914. Whether the story is true or apocryphal, there is no doubt that being led by Shackleton (when explorers were the rock stars of their day) was deemed to be very desirable. This is demonstrated by the fact that a high percentage of crew members from each expedition reapplied for the next, showing that he was able to inspire loyalty and respect from those he led.

There is a school of thought that suggests he was a reckless leader, hooked on adrenaline, and chasing personal glory at the expense of safety and common sense. However, as George Bernard Shaw once said: 'The reasonable man adapts himself to the world; the unreasonable one persists in trying to adapt the world to himself. Therefore, all progress depends on the unreasonable man.'

There is no doubt Shackleton could be classified as unreasonable in what he expected from his men, his sponsors and himself. Nevertheless, it is worth noting that his expeditions had never been done before, so the actual missions were arguably unreasonable in nature. His most famous mission, the Imperial Trans-Arctic expedition of 1914–17, took three times longer than it should. The boat got trapped in ice and had to be abandoned, but through courageous leadership (and some good fortune) all the crew returned safely. He demonstrated during the mission the essential elements all inspirational leaders possess.

Audacious visualisation was present in Shackleton from an early age; he was a dreamer who could clearly visualise further than his contemporaries. Explorers were naturally curious leaders, who pushed the boundaries of what was conceived possible. They were often naturally gifted storytellers who could inspire and persuade others to be part of their journey. Shackleton was very good at making an emotional connection (*pathos persuasion*), which was essential when he was paying minimum wage and asking people to risk their lives. As well as his persuasive skills, he was also humble enough to know he needed strong, experienced characters around him; he was comfortable letting them challenge his point of view when necessary. Everyone knew their role and was given a high degree of agency and accountability to deliver and use their specific skill sets for the good of the mission; this demonstrates *visible empowerment*. Shackleton always carried out a long, in-depth recruitment process to ensure he had the right personalities and skill sets on board. Once his men were recruited, he trusted his second in command to take care of day-to-day operational decisions. This left him free to think ahead and work on strategic rather than operational challenges.

Shackleton has gone down in history, filling the pages of many books, inspiring leaders in all walks of life. His legacy lives on, a hundred years after his death, demonstrating the importance of *inspirational leadership*.

Key takeaways
Summary

Inspirational leadership and the mantra of *better before bigger*

To instil the theory of *better before bigger* into your company, you must communicate this effectively to your colleagues and employees. Performance should be judged, and remuneration calculated, based on this mantra. If the dashboards and rewards policy are not realigned to operate around quality metrics then this transformation will take longer or, worse, not happen at all. Those you report to need to be weaned off quantity metrics by positive reinforcement on the achievement of quality-based metrics.

You also need to ensure they understand the WHY behind this switch. If you can get them to see that by being the best in your chosen categories/ markets, you will be more sustainable and dependable, giving you a competitive advantage, the transformation process will be quicker and easier.

Inspirational leadership and the paradox of *flucture*

Inspirational leadership is about knowing when to follow the playbook and when to follow your instincts. Functional managers stick to the playbook by default which, will give consistent but predictable outcomes. Inspirational leaders improvise when required, aligning with company values and mission, but not necessarily in the way expected. They know there is a need to be consistent, but also appreciate that too much predictability is not conducive to optimal performance. This balance between flexibility and structure is at the heart of the paradox of *flucture*. Visualisation, persuasion and empowerment needed to be called upon when the situation dictates, and not just at preset times and scheduled events.

An inspirational leader is equally comfortable and confident whether they are delivering an all-company vision speech, facilitating a small group workshop, or working one-to-one with a member of their team. Effective leadership is about being able to flex your style and delivery method to suit the needs of the situation.

Inspirational leadership and the concept of *embracing the plateau*

A lack of leadership training and development is one of the main factors that hold back organisational growth. We sometimes assume that just by promoting someone to a leadership position, they will simultaneously develop the required skills and mindset to deliver. A bespoke leadership training programme is required that prepares promising employees with the potential to be leaders both before they are appointed and afterwards. Leadership is complex, so the plateau period is the ideal time to work on this crucial element ahead of a period of future growth.

Inspirational leadership is needed not just at the top of an organisation but throughout it, if its full potential is going to be realised. Mature, successful organisations have multiple inspirational leaders positioned throughout them, as they know that leadership is a shared responsibility.

Reflect and commit

Before moving on to the next chapter, I would encourage you to reflect on how you could improve as a leader (and as a leadership team), so you can inspire the various stakeholders who depend on your leadership.

1 **Audacious visualisation** – Would you consider yourself skilled at articulating a vision? Currently, how good a presenter are you? i.e. can you tell a good story?

2 **Pathos persuasion** – Can you influence others to understand your point of view, and when they can't, do you have the ability to reframe or re-position this in a more effective way? i.e. can you persuade?

3 **Visible empowerment** – Do you walk your talk in front of, and alongside, your team? Do they perceive and share your passion for what you have created? i.e. do you empower?

Now based on those reflections, what are you prepared to commit to change?

I will start...
I will stop...
I will do more...
I will do less...

What's next?
Critical component #2: *Strategy clarification*

Having inspirational leaders is critical, and becomes more so, as you scale further. However, even the best leadership team will not be able to perform optimally if a clearly articulated and engaged plan is not in place. The quality of your business strategy is definitely a key success factor, and in the next chapter we will explore what an ideal strategy looks like.

5. Strategy Clarification

Mission
Coherence

Strategy
Clarification

Tactical
Agility

Offering
Relevance

Overview
Why is *strategy clarification* a core component?
Are you too focused on short-term wins?

Short-term and even medium-term success can be achieved by a combination of superior offerings and a professional, dedicated workforce. However, in isolation these two factors are not enough to sustain long-term repeatable success; they must be underpinned with an organisational level of strategic clarity. To succeed, your company needs to be crystal clear on how to outperform your competitors, rather than relying on offering or people-based advantages. However initially productive, neither of these advantages are necessarily sustainable in the same way. Strategic clarity enables you to be simultaneously more effective and more efficient in the way you operate, generating a higher return on investments and normally a more profitable business.

How adolescents normally strategise
The current problem

During the adolescent growth phase, there is a tendency for strategic decisions to become too reactive and too organic. There is a compulsion to take decisions too quickly with limited available information because we believe that reacting quickly is advantageous. External factors that may prompt this may include monitoring the strongest competitors, or customer requests. Strategy can become very organic and is too often based on those external influences, rather than determined by organisational competence and resources.

One of the reasons strategy can be both reactive and organic in nature is that leaders can become too obsessed with short-term targets. We define our success by yearly comparisons and beating internal targets. This way of operating achieves success in the short term, and sometimes medium term, but it is a very tiring way to operate. Consequently, implementing this strategy will rarely generate the highest possible net profits, as turnover and growth are prioritised over profit and sustainability.

How mature companies strategise
The ideal scenario

A mature company will have a more defined process for making strategic decisions than its adolescent counterparts. Leaders of mature companies appreciate the importance of implementing an optimal strategy to sustain longer-term success. The processes they put in place make the creation, implementation and assessment of their strategies a seamless and easily repeatable process. Therefore intentional strategic decisions are being made as opposed to the less precise, organic decisions made in less mature companies.

The result of these structured processes is that resources are used more effectively, company employees have a better understanding of their roles, and external stakeholders perceive the company as operating serenely. This positions the company as a desirable organisation both to work for and to trade with.

To achieve the desired level of strategic clarity, there are three essential elements that need to be present. However, before I outline these, I will identify some factors that should be considered when reviewing the strategic decision-making processes.

Considerations

Being able to strategise is one of the skills that separates a leader from a manager. Managers follow a plan, or a process, but are less effective when faced with a blank page or too many options. Obviously, this is a generalisation, but the ability to create, deliver and evaluate a business or departmental strategy is something that not everyone can carry out effectively. There are multiple skills needed, and a range of considerations to balance. Some leaders are naturally strategically adept, but many will require time, structure and perhaps external assistance to create something implementable.

From a competitive perspective, a company that has strategic clarity will have a significant advantage over rival companies that don't. Although they appear similar, tactics and strategy are quite different. Tactics are reactive and short term; strategy takes a considered longer-term approach. A business needs to do both well, yet most merely operate at the lower tactical level because it is less challenging, and therefore less intimidating. Successful, mature businesses take the next step into more advanced strategic thinking.

Strategic rather than operational
Going wider and deeper

The word strategy holds military connotations, as one of the key elements that are considered during conflict. The military objective is to derive and deliver a strategy that enables an armed force to succeed over its enemies. While competing in business may not hold the same peril, the same logic can be applied, i.e. how can you beat competition given your circumstances and the resources at your disposal? The quality and time given to strategic planning is something that certainly differentiates effective companies from their competitors. Military history demonstrates how smaller, more organised forces have managed to defeat larger, yet strategically naïve, armies. One of the best-known examples is the Battle of Agincourt in 1415 when a depleted English army of 3,000 troops managed to defeat a French army of over 30,000, who also had the 'advantage' of cavalry and heavy infantry. The victory was achieved by a combination of better tactics (the English used a bow and arrow attack to disrupt the French and to nullify the cavalry), better use of the conditions (the French became bogged down in the mud with heavier armoury to manoeuvre) and inspiring leadership (Henry V led from the front when it came to the hand-to-hand combat). This example demonstrates that the appropriate amount of time and brainpower should be allocated in advance to ensure thorough understanding of possible scenarios, so the optimal strategy can be selected.

A chess grandmaster will spend the maximum time available working through future scenarios before making their move. Strategic thought is more advanced than operational thinking, being both wider and deeper. It considers more factors and accepts that immediate losses may sometimes be necessary to achieve a far greater victory.

Operational thinking wins the battle; strategic thought wins the war. These different objectives make it challenging to have strategic-level discussions with employees, who spend 90 per cent of their time on operational-level activities. Therefore, ambitious leaders will require a board, a business coach or a non-executive director to provide a sounding board who can debate these strategic decisions.

Planning ahead
Pulling back to see further

Strategic thinking represents visualising the future and requires you to consider what your business may come to face, and how you can best prepare for this. As we know, situations evolve and change, but there are patterns, trends and scenarios that can be analysed to better inform of us for future requirements.

Large tech and pharmaceutical companies spend much of their past profits each year on research and development to ensure the best chance of future success. Forward thinking, scenario planning and market research are built into business operations. Establishing research and development as a core part of your business will be vital in growing your organisation from adolescence to maturity. Mature companies constantly consider both the current and future needs of their customers, suppliers and market as a whole. Their financial plans will focus on the next three to five years, not just the next three to five quarters. Their investment strategy will be based on generating a return of investment over a number of quarters, and not just the next few weeks. They will also have an internal training function that develops employees and leaders who possess the skill sets the business requires in the future.

Once this mindset is embedded into an organisation, it gives the company greater strategic agility, giving them options that have been considered, costed and resourced in advance. If needed these can be implemented more quickly than by their competitors, who have become too focused on day-to-day operations.

There are numerous examples of established companies that have been put into liquidation because of their lack of strategic thinking and a belief that the status quo was unchanging. They were blind-sided by more agile competitors. Consider what you would do as a business if your 'best' customers/employees/suppliers left you tomorrow.

Challenge yourself and your leadership team to stand back from the business regularly to enable you to see further ahead and gain a wider viewpoint. Being too close to something doesn't allow you a great, objective perspective. It only enables you to consider the here and now.

Optimal complexity
Are we challenging ourselves enough or too much?

Strategy is all about finding the optimal balance; if you come up with something that is too complex to actually implement, you fail. On the other hand, if you generate something that is too simple to give you a competitive advantage, you also fail. The mantra you must remember is: complex enough to challenge, but simple enough deliver.

'Complex enough' means something that is difficult for competitors to copy, giving you a distinct advantage over them. This might be a quicker service, or a more convenient way for your customers to receive your product, but it needs to be something the customer values. Obviously, with increasing competition, it can be very hard to generate a genuine competitive advantage for any length of time. Competitors will be able to create similar offerings or products relatively quickly. Therefore strategic thinking needs to be constant, rather than occasional. What seemed like ground-breaking thinking soon becomes the norm, so the more complex your solution, the longer it will take for others to catch up.

On the flip side, you also require the ability to consistently implement your strategy, often across multiple locations, so the more complex you make something, the harder it is to deliver consistently. If the captains on the battlefield don't fully understand their general's strategic plan, then the chances are the implementation is going to be poor and the battle lost.

Strategies and strategic plans need to be inherently fit for purpose and implementable. If either characteristic is missing, then the optimal outcome will not be achieved.

Essential elements & desirable attributes

1. Mission coherence
How clear are we on our why, what and how?

Many new businesses start out when an entrepreneur sees a gap in the market, having the foresight and drive to exploit it. This represents an opportunistic beginning. Either way, there is a large degree of opportunism in the way they build their business. However, as they mature and become a more dominant player in their chosen market, some of this opportunism needs to be replaced by a more strategic intent. *Mission coherence* is about ensuring you have the optimal strategy in place for the next phase of growth. Coherence is needed around your core commitments, your resources, and your abilities as an organisation. To mature, you must have a disciplined approach to both the formation and implementation of strategy across your business, as the stakes are ever increasing. Yes, you have more to gain, but conversely, you also have more to lose. If coherence is going to be achieved, the leader must have the detachment to make objective decisions about what stays and what goes.

The logic and consistency needed here is achieved by focusing on and embedding three specific attributes:

i.   company competencies

ii. balancing the need to farm and the desire to hunt

iii. choosing your battles.

i. Company competencies
Are we playing to our strengths?

Simply put, this is what you do well as a company. Whilst the average company may claim to be good in all areas of production, delivery and servicing of customers, the reality is most companies have pockets of real strength which they should build their offering around. It may be a signature product range with innovative features, it could be quick customer service, or it could be their technical expertise in a certain field. Whatever your company competencies are, an effective strategy needs to be developed to maximise them. You need to make sure your competencies are at the forefront of not only the brand identity, but also the way you intend to scale your business to maturity. That means a competency can't be a person, as they are difficult to scale, and may possibly leave your business at some point in the future.

The concept of core competencies was first introduced by C.K. Prahalad and Gary Hamel (see their 1990 article 'The core competence of the corporation' in *Harvard Business Review*), who described them as 'a harmonized combination of multiple skills that distinguish a firm in the marketplace and are the foundation of company competitiveness'. They gave three specific criteria for defining a competency:

1   provides potential access to a wide variety of markets

2   makes a significant contribution to the perceived benefits of the end product

3   difficult to imitate by competitors.

For instance, Honda's competency is making great engines; Apple's is designing visually appealing tech products; in the case of McDonald's it is their production system. Considering your company competencies facilitates objective thought about what they currently are and, more importantly, what they need to be as you scale your company. Are you focusing investment on something that merely copies what others are doing? Or have you created something that benefits your customers in a new way?

During a phase of high and consistent growth, leaders can fall into the trap of putting all their investment, and focusing all their resources, on the here and now. This focus is understandable in one respect, as it will probably maximise the profits generated in the short term. However, the downside to this approach is that not enough resources or focus is given to research and development of new products, new ways to service customers and new technology. None of these expenditures will give you any return of investment in the short term, but without this more balanced approach you may suffer declining profits and market share in the future. Competitors may bring out quicker, cheaper or better versions of your current offerings. Your company competencies, once identified, need to be continually invested in if they are going to remain vital. If you feel there is no longevity in your current competencies, then you need to start creating or potentially acquiring new ones. The question of whether a core competency remains as such is one a good leader should ask regularly.

ii. Farming vs hunting
How do we balance these contrasting strategies?

The second attribute that has a direct impact on company strategy is the choice between 'hunting', 'farming' or balancing the two. 'Hunting' represents continually seeking new customers; 'farming' represents increasing the spend and profits from existing customers.

It is probable, but not always true, that during a high-growth phase the focus on farming existing customers can become a secondary consideration behind the desire to hunt new ones. The number of new customers or contracts won can become a vanity metric for some companies. Without consciously doing so it is possible to create a large and investment-heavy sales arm, which will mean you need to continually find lots of new customers to justify this investment. If this is the case, it is also possible that maximising returns from existing customers has not been given the resources and focus that it perhaps should. This may happen because it is organisationally difficult to prioritise farming and hunting at the same time.

Although difficult, it is essential that to move from adolescence to maturity, a company both farms and hunts successfully. If you are not farming your existing customer base effectively, you are not maximising the potential profits you could be generating from them. As well as this, you are probably not giving them enough love and attention for them to stay customers. The widely quoted statistic is that it's five times cheaper to keep an existing customer than it is to find a new one. Whether this is strictly precise, given the lowering costs of digital marketing and onboarding, the basic premise remains true. Protecting and maintaining our existing market share should always be job number one, otherwise any successful hunting strategy will merely be replacing customers we are already losing, rather than growing our customer base and market share.

Similarly, if we don't retain and reward our existing team, we will have to spend more money on recruitment, and also lose the experience and company knowhow they have. In this respect, our people strategy should mirror our customer strategy by finding the optimal balance between farming and hunting.

Any business strategy that doesn't contain a clear commitment to enhance the experience of both existing customers and team members is lacking a crucial element.

iii. Choosing your battles
Where should we focus our resources and efforts?

The final attribute is having a good strategy with clearly defined markets or fields that you intend to compete in. It is important that this choice is based on future opportunities rather than past successes. Just because you have previously been successful in a market, there is no guarantee of future success. You need to realistically assess both the potential of the market in the future, and your ability to compete in that market. Given that every company has finite resources (both human and financial), decisions need to be taken (usually annually) about the offerings and markets you wish to target, and the resources allocated to each one. In the same way, a general must decide how many troops and what skilled regiments to employ to any specific battle as part of the overall war.

Strategic focus is the key to future profitability. Generally, it is more profitable to be one of the dominant players in a smaller market than it is to be less dominant in a larger one. If you are a non-dominant player, the strategy, tactics and needs of the market you inhabit are not established by you, but by the dominant players and the market itself. This means your strategy must be reactive rather than proactive. On the other hand, if you establish a dominant position in a more niche market, you are in greater control of your future and you can introduce a proactive strategy that will enable you to maintain, and ideally increase, your market share.

As with all strategy-based decisions there are no right or wrong answers. If there were, everyone would be doing the same thing. It is about objective assessment and working primarily with supporting data, with a little bit of intuition thrown in. The more you know about your customers, your competitors and your own competencies, the better the strategic decisions you can make.

Once you've chosen your strategy and made the commitments, it comes down to regular evaluation of whether your strategic choices are delivering the returns you predicted. If not, you may need to pivot.

2. Offering relevance
Where and how are we going to compete?

The second essential element of *strategic clarification* is confirming where you are going to compete, and how you are going to do this. When it comes to deciding 'where', it is essential you understand the term 'table stakes'. A table stake is the investment a stakeholder must make just to earn a place at the table. Simply stated, it is used to identify and quantify the minimum entry requirement to enter a given market. The logic being if you don't satisfy those minimum requirements you can't play in that market. A table stake could be a price point, or a certain technology or a specific cost model, without which you won't have a credible starting position or a way of competing. Once you have met the minimum requirements to play in that market, you then decide how you are going to establish a competitive advantage. It is about ensuring your offerings have relevance to their audience. Using simple marketing language, offerings either need to add pleasure or remove pain. The greater the fit between their need and your offering, the higher the relevance, which should result in better sales and profits, all other factors being equal.

To ensure you have a high degree of *offering relevance* you will need to be crystal clear on these three attributes:

i. your default strategy

ii. your defendable base

iii. maintainable differentiation.

i. Your default strategy
Low cost or differentiation?

In reality, a minority of businesses possess either a lower cost production or service capability than their rivals; therefore adopting a strategy based on having the lowest cost is neither realistic nor advisable. There can be only one player in the market with the cheapest cost basis (think Ryanair in the short-haul flight market, or Lidl in the supermarket sector) and to dislodge them you will need to consistently undercut them. Unless you're confident that you are going to be the cheapest in your market (or market niche), then competing in this way is very risky. The danger is that you may not win that race and coming second will leave you with little profit and very few strategic alternatives.

The global brands that choose to compete in this way, such as IKEA or Lidl, have deep pockets and have embedded their cost or purchasing advantage into their operations to ensure sustainability. Being the cheapest service provider generally requires a cheaper source of labour than your competitors. In most Western countries this is difficult to achieve, given the freedom of movement across borders and legislation surrounding minimum wages. Having a cheaper production cost is similarly hard to maintain unless you own the machinery or already have the knowhow within your business. Most consumables are cheaply produced in the same or similar factories in the developing world which are equally accessible to all companies. Gaining a competitive advantage this way can be very challenging to achieve.

When entering a new market you may need to be the lowest-cost option to get customers to switch from their existing provider (this often happens in the mobile phone industry), but this can only be at best a temporary strategy to gain market share; this is unless you have a genuine lower-cost production or service advantage over your rivals. Consequently, by default, the majority of companies will need to pursue a differentiation-based business strategy, as this has less risk attached and allows greater flexibility to compete.

ii. Your defendable base(s)
How secure is what you already have?

Attributes of good strategic decision-making can be found in the board game Risk. The goal of the game is simple: world domination. To take countries from your opponents, thus eliminating them from the map until you end up occupying all territories. While I am not suggesting that either this level of aggression or world domination should be part of your current business strategy, as in Risk I would advocate you create a firm stronghold. Spread your troops (or your resources) too thinly or try to accelerate too swiftly and this will leave you open to counterattack and ultimately defeat. The lesson to be learnt here is to make sure you are expanding from a strong base, which is defendable if competitors try to compete directly with you. A good business strategy will be centred on how you maintain and increase the revenue (and profits) you generate from your existing customers. If you are not maximising return from your existing customers, why would you invest your finite resources in generating new ones? Developing new services and offerings to create additional income streams, building on established relationships with existing customers, is more strategically logical. This makes more sense than entering a completely new market or trying to onboard new customers.

This can all be traced back to having clarity on your core company competencies and building your growth strategy around these. Operating in this way will result in more efficiency with your resources, assisting you to differentiate your offering from competitors, and aligning you with the needs of your target market, giving you a firm and loyal customer base to expand from.

Knowing the quality of resources needed to maintain and farm your existing customers enables you to work out what can be allocated to the riskier task of finding new customers and new markets. Having a defendable, and relatively predictable, baseline of turnover and profits will give you the confidence to be more aggressive in your business acquisition strategy, as you work from a stronger starting position. As in Risk, establishing a strong defendable base is always a good strategic starting point.

iii. Maintainable differentiation

Have we created the capacity to maintain the competitive advantages we have achieved?

Differentiation can come in a multitude of ways. You can have more bells and whistles, provide a quicker service, give the customers the opportunity to create their own offering, build a service-on-demand structure, and many more variations. Most of the time, it will be a combination of these that will prove to be most effective. The combination you choose will be generally based on two factors, first your business's core competencies, and second what these competitors offer. The most successful companies are simultaneously able to negate or match the offering of the main competitors, while also offering their customers an additional unique feature or two on their service or product.

The challenge is not only creating these differentiating features, but also maintaining that differentiated offering. Most features are relatively easy for competitors to match or even surpass in time. Take mobile phones as an example; when Apple brought out its first iPhone with a touchscreen, its competitive advantage lasted approximately six months before its main competitors developed models with the same capability. The obvious conclusion is that innovation and product/service development need to be a constant and ingrained part of your business, not a random occurrence.

The other factor to consider, which can often get lost in the day-to-day operations of fast-growing companies, is that true differentiation is decided by your customers and the market as a whole. We often have a false sense of how unique our service or products in the eyes of our customers. As *Purple Cow* author Seth Godin observes, the goal for all companies is to create a remarkable product or service that will not only grab people's attention, but is so remarkable they tell their friends, family and colleagues about it. Godin suggests companies should set up their own 'purple cow' innovation work streams to ensure a constant focus on producing a flow of remarkable products and services. This advice has been successfully embedded in tech companies like Google, Apple and Microsoft, which is part of the reason they have managed to remain market leaders over a number of decades. The challenge is implementing this when you are a fast-growing adolescent company, focusing on day-to-day challenges. This is why it must be a strategic decision made at the top of the organisation, to ensure it gets the necessary resources and attention.

A differentiation strategy can't be a short-term project. The mentality must be part of company culture and embedded in its operations if potential scaling is to be achieved.

3. Tactical agility
Same again?

The reason McDonald's has become the largest franchise business in the world is not based on the quality of the products they provide (these are just the table stakes in their sector), but around the predictability and efficiency of the operational processes. Through years of testing and tweaking, they have created a formidable operating system, which enables them to set up franchises anywhere in the world, instantly producing a consistent and predictable offering to millions of customers.

As I mentioned before, it was not the founders of McDonald's that established this predictable process, but salesman Ray Kroc. What Kroc knew was that any good business strategy is built on predictable processes, and without this element, the generated profits would be far more inconsistent.

To ensure the maximum *tactical agility* is achievable there are three specific attributes that are ideally present:

i.   measuring against expectations

ii. minimal viable products

iii. pivoting.

i. Measuring success in advance
Have we decided what success looks like?

To deem something as successful there need to be some expectations to measure performance against. Without this, success or failure is just a subjective viewpoint. There are not inherently good or bad strategies, there are just strategies that will be judged at some predetermined point as being successful or not. When someone says they have a good idea, what they really mean is that they have an idea that from their perspective, and based on their desired outcome, seems good to them. From a five-year old's viewpoint, quickly eating as many chocolates as possible seems like a really good strategy, but if you're the parent, or even the child later that day, it probably seems a flawed strategy. The point is, without jointly agreed expectations laid out in advance, it is not possible to objectively conclude whether a given strategy is working or not.

When businesses create their overall strategy, a key attribute that needs to be present is clear expectations. Not only do the expectations need to be clear, but the method of calculations also must be preset. Likewise, the cut-off points, where the strategy is deemed to be failing, need to be set ahead of implementation. All these elements are far easier to agree on, and set before commencement, when there is less emotion and sunk cost involved. If you don't set these in advance, you risk very emotionally charged and unproductive strategy review sessions down the line, where everyone involved will have a different view of what constitutes success.

The US Army have embedded After Action Reviews (AARs) into their operations and these have since been adopted by commercial companies as a way of assessing performance in a specific area of the business. An AAR is distinct from a standard project debrief in that it begins with a clear comparison of intended and actual results achieved. An external facilitator or consultant is used to bring greater objectivity. While primarily focused on the degree of success, they will also discuss lessons to be learnt as a way of informing changes for the future operational strategy.

ii. Minimal viable products
First impression?

The concept of creating a minimum viable product (MVP) to test the appetite of current or potential customers for a new offering was first used in software and design agencies but has now been widely adopted by the business world. Originally applied to the creation of a product, it can also be used in service settings as well. The logic is that, as part of the process of creating a new offering, you should get a basic version of the proposed offering into a test environment as soon as possible. This enables you to see the initial reaction before you invest too much time and resources in creating a more advanced version. In the past, a company would spend a lot of time and effort finishing, crafting and polishing any offering before releasing it. The problem with this approach is that with so much investment ahead of launch, it makes it much more difficult to objectively judge the quality of a new product or service. You need it to work to get the investment back and profit further. There's so much emotional investment made in advance, the company is sometimes unable to process constructive feedback and will carry on regardless. By using MVPs as part of your strategic process, you are less invested, so it's easier to either go back to the drawing board or abandon an idea altogether.

Today's markets are ever evolving and the production cost and speed of bringing new products to market has reduced. Therefore companies need to be more agile in their strategic approach. They need to respond not only to feedback from initial adopters, but also respond to competitors' offerings quickly. These twin demands underpin the need for developing MVPs and having MVPs as an integral part of the strategy process.

Many companies will use their most loyal customers as the test group, as their feedback is more relevant and they are better equipped to judge whether a proposed product or service is aligned with the business vision and values. Releasing MVPs for feedback may seem daunting to more conservative companies, but this strategy is necessary to keep pace in modern markets and grow effectively.

iii. Pivoting
Have we built a cruise liner or a speedboat?

Previously, companies who had gained a competitive advantage by either being the first mover, or by creating an innovative new offering, would enjoy a relatively long period of dominance and profit. But given the speed with which other companies can now create a similar offering, or replicate any competitive advantage, the ability to pivot becomes a desirable attribute.

There is a balance to be achieved here between having the ability to pivot, i.e. make changes as and when circumstances dictate, and maintaining your chosen course. If you pivot too frequently you risk confusing yourself and your stakeholders about what direction you are truly heading in. This confusion will negatively impact confidence and may result in a loss of momentum. However, if you refuse to pivot, adhering to your strategy rigidly even if it becomes less appropriate, you will not create the optimal outcomes for your stakeholders.

The key here is to differentiate between strategy and tactics again. Pivoting strategy should be rare, occurring only when major changes in circumstance happen, or it becomes clear the current strategy is consistently inadequate for the required outcomes. In contrast, pivoting tactics is something that should be considered more frequently. If we equate the strategy to the overarching plan, and the tactics to our specific actions, it's logical to assume that tactics should be more agile than strategy.

Tactics relate to the pricing, positioning and overall proposition, all of which need to be considered against your competitors' offerings and market conditions. If you don't empower your team to change tactics as and when required, then you hamper their ability to compete. While *tactical agility* becomes necessary as competition increases and marketing time for new offerings reduces simultaneously, strategic rigidity can also be a desirable attribute. Having a well-considered and resourced plan to follow can give you a competitive advantage over a more random and reactive competitor.

In summary, I advocate that with strategy you should be more like a cruise liner that varies very little from its preset destination, and with tactics, be more like a speedboat with the ability to change course quickly, and when required to take advantage of new conditions or opportunities. So ideally, build a speed liner!

Case study

Greggs

:: GREGGS

An overnight success story in 20 years may sound like a contradiction, but this is what the bakery store Greggs has managed to achieve. Greggs has accelerated its growth in the past two decades by putting in place a strategic expansion plan based around acquisition. This came after 80 years of slower, more organic growth, making its change in approach all the more admirable. They are a great example of a company that is aligned, by staying true to their heritage and values, and transparent, by maintaining strong communications channels with all stakeholders. Their strategic choices have also demonstrated considerable vulnerability by expanding outside of their heartland and core product range.

Greggs have a very clearly stated mission that has evolved as their reputation and reach have increased. They now perceive themselves as a nationwide brand serving the mass market and have ambitions to become the customers favourite for food-on-the-go. Their approach is rooted in a clear mission that aligns with their values, demonstrating effective *mission coherence*. They understand what their core competencies are (serving quality instant food) and have managed to increase their sales in existing markets. As well as this, they have moved into new markets (the south of the UK) with new offerings, including vegan alternatives. This dual strategy has enabled them to grow both market share and spend-per-head over the last few years. As a company, they realise the importance of supplying *relevant offerings* to their ever-expanding market, hence the move into vegetarian and vegan products, as more people adopt this lifestyle. They have also focused on acquiring and subsequently expanding their own supply chain, so they can tailor to their customer needs, and take further control of the quality of their offering. This control combined with the lower cost base, has been established by owning their own means of production. Therefore, they can offer higher quality products at lower costs than most of the direct competitors; this presents them with a clear competitive advantage from which they can grow.

Greggs strategy also exhibits *tactical agility* by trying new products in suitable markets. If these inventions do well, they have the capacity to increase supply across their outlets quickly. They have generated a trusted customer base, who can offer them instant feedback and insight via their loyalty app. This enables them to pivot very quickly if necessary, further adding to the company's *tactical agility.*

Strategic clarification is about reliably keeping to your commitments and making sure all stakeholders are on board with both your mission and strategy. Greggs has satisfied all of its primary stakeholder groups, inspiring high levels of customer loyalty, with healthy staff retention, and a share price that has increased by 60 per cent in the last ten years, far outstripping the market average. In a crowded market sector, their clarity of strategic leadership has given all customers, employees and shareholders an admirable return, which doesn't seem likely to change anytime soon.

Key takeaways

Summary

Strategy clarification **and the mantra of** *better before bigger*

The strategic mantra *better before bigger* is valid and applicable when survival and growth are the goals in adolescence, but this needs to be replaced with a more refined version that focuses on choosing the optimal strategic options to mature for long-term sustainability. For this to occur there must be a degree of detachment applied to what has happened so far; you need to be comfortable adjusting your aim from getting bigger to becoming the best in your chosen market. Best has permanence; biggest doesn't. Best is more within your control; biggest depends more on external factors. By switching emphasis you will be giving yourself the reason and the opportunity to re-evaluate your current strategic thinking and operational structures. While they may both have been aligned to the goal of getting bigger, one (or both) may not be appropriate if the new goal is to be the best in your sector.

Mature companies may be seen simultaneously as both the best and biggest player in their niche, but it is important to understand that they became the biggest by being the best. The reverse cannot be applied: you can't become the best merely by being the biggest. Aiming for maximum quality brings simplicity to the strategic decisions you need to make. It will liberate your thinking once the commitment has been made.

Strategy clarification **and the paradox of** *flucture*

In my experience, most adolescent stage companies don't have a robust and/or defined strategic process in place. They don't yet have the internal discipline to create, implement and review strategy in a consistent and repeatable manner. In short, they are too fluid (flexible) in their approach.

Adolescent businesses are often too bogged down in operational activities, or do not have the required skill sets to strategise effectively. They assume that a clear, engaged strategy is exclusive to larger companies. What they don't realise is these bigger organisations only gained their influential positions by considering strategy thoroughly. Adolescent companies must ring-fence the required time to strategise; this must be implemented by the leadership team. This structured approach requires the development or acquisition of forward-thinking people.

Strategy clarification and the
concept of *embracing the plateau*

A reduction of your current growth rate in the short term could be an outcome of *embracing the plateau.* This period of consideration is going to serve you and your company by adding more resilience, greater clarity and enhanced sustainability. However, these are not short-term outputs. To adopt this mindset, with the level of commitment required, you must have the courage to place your future vision of the company perhaps ahead of the current needs of stakeholders.

Embracing the plateau is not a quick-win strategy. It is probable that re-evaluating the way you operate may generate some difficult decisions; leaders need to be comfortable with this consequence. You need to be comfortable being uncomfortable while the new strategic thinking is embedded across the company. This circles back to having clarity on your 'why' and being able to articulate a revised vision – *pathos persuasion* in action.

Reflect and commit

Before moving on to the next chapter, I would encourage you to reflect on how you could increase clarity to the way your strategy is generated, communicated, implemented and reviewed. How can you make this a more intentional and less organic process?

1 **Mission coherence** – does your strategy fully utilise your core competencies, whilst having a good balance between retaining existing customer/clients and finding new ones?

2 **Offering relevance** – have you created something which is genuinely differentiated from the competition? Are you able to maintain or ideally increase that differentiation in the future?

3 **Tactical agility** – do you have enough feedback loops in place to give an early indication of how well offerings are being received, so that you know when to increase investment, and when you need to pivot?

Now based on those reflections, what are you prepared to commit to change?

I will start...
I will stop...
I will do more...
I will do less...

What's next?
Critical component #3: *Stakeholder reciprocation*

The leaders of mature companies can not only develop commercially viable strategies, which give them a distinct competitive advantage, but also know how to get their key stakeholders on board. They understand the importance of working collaboratively with various groups; I will be explaining how they do this in the next chapter.

6. Stakeholder Reciprocation

Overview

Why is *stakeholder reciprocation* a core component?
Are you considering the needs of all your stakeholders?

As your business grows, it is very important that the breadth and depth of your relationships with each stakeholder group grow consistently and, ideally, quickly. The quality of these relationships is a crucial cornerstone of the foundations that you can scale your business on. If any of these relationships are unstable or founded on unaligned values or vision, it will make future growth less certain.

By stakeholders I mean any group of individuals that are reliant upon or invested in your business. These will normally comprise the following four distinct groups:

1 employees

2 customers or clients

3 associates/suppliers

4 shareholders.

There can be other groups like commercial lenders, partner organisations or local communities which some companies need to consider as well.

The key to improving the quality of any relationship is all about moving it from one based on responsibility to one of accountability. If we look at our strongest relationship, either personal or in business, underpinning this relationship is high accountability; both parties have a strong sense of their duty to the other. Being accountable not only means being responsible for something, but also being able to justify your actions. The fact that you are answerable increases both the stakes and the commitment. If you already have a high degree of accountability across the business then all is good; if not, it is crucial this is prioritised.

How adolescents tend to relate – the current challenge

The main difference between adolescent companies and their mature counterparts is that the former can tend to concentrate on transactional elements of the relationship. An adolescent company may want to win each transaction, which demonstrates short-term thinking, and often puts the needs of one stakeholder group above the need of others. An example of this can be found with supermarkets and their suppliers. Supermarkets inhabit the dominant position and squeeze their suppliers to maximise the return to their investors. This is one reason why many of the supermarkets are still adolescent businesses, or at least acting as such. This is often referred to as a win/lose mentality and is a very binary way of relating. A more enlightened mentality of win/win, where both parties come away equally satisfied, is of course preferable.

How mature companies relate – the ideal scenario

Mature companies are constructed around intentional relationships, rather than the organic kind found in their adolescent counterparts. During the high-growth phase, the quality of relationships is often disregarded. There has also been a lack of consideration for developing strategies to strengthen and deepen stakeholder relationships. There may be a lack of a strategy for maximising those relationships. This lack of focus and absence of strategic thinking will result in a very varied set of stakeholders within each group, making business operations more complicated. This complication is generated by having a wide variety of stakeholder expectations and an inconsistent opinion within each group about the ideal relationship. In simple terms, you need to satisfy, and ideally delight, too many subsets of stakeholders simultaneously. Before you get any bigger, you must align your offerings with the expectations and needs of your ideal members within each group, the key word being 'ideal'.

➤ Do you have an offering that your customers love?

➤ Do you have a company culture that attracts and retains the best talent?

➤ Do you have partners that support and respond when required?

➤ Do you have shareholders who really understand you and the business?

It comes down to simply devoting enough time to each group and creating a mutual, pre-agreed set of desirables outcomes for both parties.

Considerations

Being able to rely upon and, when required, leverage existing relationships is critical when you are looking to scale. Although they don't appear on your balance sheet, relationships are every bit as important as your financial assets. If you don't have the support and trust of the different stakeholder groups as you work through a transformation phase, making the required changes is going to be that much harder.

Whereas connections are perceived as the new currency, particularly for freelancers, relationships have probably always been a currency for businesses. It may be that you haven't thought of them in these terms until now. It also may be that you currently don't have the required strategies to maximise those relationships or establish better ones in place. Whether you look to upgrade existing relationships or start new ones, there are three key considerations to keep in mind.

i. Reciprocation must be present
Is it all about me, them, or us?

Reciprocation can simply be defined as mutual giving or receiving, or more elaborately as a committed long-lasting relationship where both partners continue to nurture feelings of respect for each other. Reciprocity is developed and woven into relationships sometimes without the participants' conscious input. The simple definition above is the absolute minimum level you should look to implement, whereas the more complex one would be the ideal. Either way, the unchanging factor is that the relationship must be two way. For this to happen, both parties need to appreciate the other's position. They need to put themselves in the other's shoes. Specifically, the key attributes that need to be known and discussed are:

The 'WHY' – an agreed mission or vision
All strong relationships are built around a shared mission or vision. The two parties must have a matching outcome they would like to achieve, otherwise one party will feel the relationship is heading in the wrong direction. Spending time discussing, agreeing and ideally committing to the shared outcome in advance of the relationship is the ideal scenario.
Why are we working together?

The 'WHAT' – a pre-agreed common language and ideal behaviours

It may sound obvious, but sometimes the language we use can alienate the other person in the relationship or at least make it difficult for them to contribute at the same level. A good example is the financial information a company chooses to share with its shareholders and team members. If too much technical language is present, or the figures are positioned in the wrong context, it may be difficult for some stakeholders to contribute. Similarly, if a company uses too much industry jargon and too many acronyms in its marketing communication, it may alienate existing and potential customers.

Agreeing the behaviours you expect to see from each other is equally essential. Different companies and stakeholder groups will have varying standards and principles. Therefore agreeing a common set will make for a smoother experience for both parties and reduce the chance of misunderstandings.

What do you expect from others, and what can they expect from you?

The 'HOW' – success outcomes

Linked to having a shared desirable outcome (the 'why'), is both parties being clear about, and motivated by, the rewards they will receive once their goals are achieved. Each party may receive different rewards from success, but all must possess the same success criteria. For instance, if a company works with an influencer marketer, the company may receive thousands more hits on its website, or more enquiries for its product as the reward. In return, the influencer would receive free products or payment for the same success criteria being achieved. Both parties win, but have different rewards.

What does success look like for each of your key stakeholder relationships?

ii. Trust credits

Do you have enough credits in your various accounts?

As I briefly discussed in Chapter 4, trust is a basic element of any human relationship. It is also an essential ingredient in business to build a long-term, mutually beneficial relationship. When a high degree of trust is present, both parties can focus all their time and effort on how best to achieve the defined goal (which is the second key element). If trust is not present, then both parties will spend unnecessary time focusing on what the other party is or is not doing. They will obsess about how their partner is behaving by double-checking the information and figures they have given, thus working unproductively.

It's easy to see if insufficient trust is in place. If you do not trust your employees thoroughly, you will waste time micromanaging them. Similarly, if you do not trust your suppliers, your dialogues with them will be complicated by your desire to check the information they give you. High trust enables companies to operate with confidence and certainty.

I like to think of trust as a currency rather than a static state, hence the reference to credits. Trust credits work like a bank account, in that you need to pay in before you can withdraw. The ideal situation is that you build up a number of credits with each stakeholder by fulfilling promises by the set date. Once these credits are built up, if in the future for some reason you don't deliver on the agreement or against the pre-agreed expectations, you are unlikely to lose that relationship. Instead, you will just use up some of the 'trust credits' you have acquired. The more severe the under-delivery, the more credits you will have to spend.

The concept of 'trust credits' is relevant without us realising it in most of our everyday relationships but is seldom considered in commercial relationships. Think about your key stakeholder relationships: could you say which ones are in the black and which may be close to going overdrawn? Do you know with each one how to improve the state of the 'trust bank balance?'

iii. Radical transparency
Time to get naked

All companies have finite resources, whether we are talking time, money or attention. Therefore if you allocate too much of a single resource to improve one specific relationship, it has to come out of the total amount you can allocate to the others. The most obvious example of this comes at the end of the financial year. This is when a CEO (and their board) must decide what to do with the net profits the company has generated. The decisions about how much to pay in dividends to keep shareholders happy, how much to put aside for pay rises and bonuses to keep employees motivated, how much to put aside for research and development to create new products and services to retain customers, and how much to invest in your partner relationships must be taken.

While it can be tricky to balance the potentially competing expectations of different groups, pre-agreements with each group can make this process far easier to navigate. For instance, if your employees expect a pay rise each year at inflation levels or higher you can build this into your financial calculations. Similarly, if you have agreed with any shareholders or investors that you will give them a set percentage return on their investment each year, this figure can also be calculated in advance. This gives clarity on how much is potentially available to offer other stakeholder groups.

The next level of transparency I would recommend is letting your shareholders/investors know your thinking behind resource allocation. They may not always agree with your reasoning, but your transparency is enough to build additional trust, and therefore respect, into the relationship.

If you can't afford to give pay rises during a given period as profits may be lower than expected, be transparent and empower the employees to assist you in building the profits back up so the pay rises can then be made. If you need to increase prices to your customers, because there has been a growth in the cost of your raw materials, let them know why.

If you have onboarded stakeholders that are aligned with your core commitments and are therefore interested in the medium-to-long-term success of your business, they will appreciate this higher level of transparency. If you think about the highest quality and most long-lasting relationship you've had, I would guess that these have been the most transparent.

Essential elements & desirable attributes

To transform your adolescent business into an autonomous mature company, there are three essential elements that you need to embed into company culture.

1. Authentic engagement
Keep the destination in focus

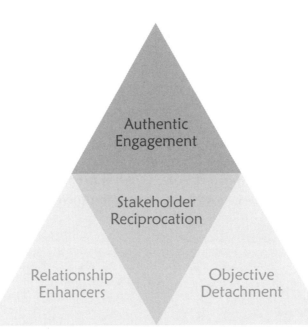

Did you know that if an aeroplane is flying from London to New York it is off course for 90 per cent of the flight? Most flight paths are continually updated during the flight, to adjust to external conditions. However, the one thing that remains constant is their end destination.

The best companies are driven by leaders who display similar traits to an aeroplane navigation system, namely that they keep their end destination as their primary objective and make rational not emotional decisions. This first element of *stakeholder reciprocation* is ensuring your relationships are built with consideration to your core commitments and, more specifically, to your values and culture.

The engagement you have with the stakeholders must be genuinely reciprocal. Each new relationship you bring on (or existing one you renew) needs to be as close as possible to the ideal persona for that stakeholder group. There can be no unnecessary passengers on your flight if you are going to reach your destination on time.

Let's break this down to the attributes you (and your leadership team) should operate with to achieve this *authentic engagement*:

i.   putting values before needs

ii. understanding before being understood

iii. rigorous onboarding processes.

i. Putting values before needs
Are you shopping hungry?

One of the questions I ask my clients when they are experiencing a challenging relationship is whether they're guilty of 'shopping hungry?' This means they are putting their needs ahead of their values. If you were walking round a supermarket while starving hungry, this might result in buying a random item to satisfy this hunger, regardless of your preferences.

This analogy has many parallels in a business environment. Perhaps the most important is the necessity of clarity on the values and traits you require in the stakeholders that you work with. In my experience, not enough businesses are clear and resolute on their values and traits with regards to their various stakeholder relationships. They therefore end up with suboptimal relationships, meaning they have employees who don't align with the company ethos, clients and customers who are high maintenance and provide a negative return on investment, and partners who don't provide the expected quality of service. All of these suboptimal relationships can impact your business financially and culturally every day.

The solution is simple. Step one is to generate clarity. Get clear on the values and behavioural traits that are important to you, which must be present in the stakeholders you work with. Step two is to effectively communicate. Communicate these values and traits across the business so that everyone agrees and aligns with them. Step three is simply to commit. Create processes and systems that allow you to monitor and assess whether both potential, and current, stakeholders are demonstrating these values.

Implementing these steps means proactive leadership is required from the top of the company. If you compromise on them, you send the wrong message to the rest of the company that your current set of requirements are optimal rather than non-negotiable. Yes, it might take longer to fill the vacancies this leaves, and consequently may have a negative impact on the business in the short term. However, recruiting the 'right' employees is key to medium and long-term success, which is where you should focus as leader. This may mean that you need to have frank conversations with existing partners or suppliers who are not working to your values. Although daunting, you will often find that this honest conversation receives a more positive reaction than expected, and you end up with a stronger relationship afterwards.

A company that is clear on its purpose and values can communicate them well, and has strength of character to commit to them on a daily basis, is respected and attractive. Similarly, employees admire leaders who demonstrate clarity, communication and commitment.

As you look across your business, can you see examples of either purchases or appointments which you have made that, with the benefit of hindsight, demonstrate that you were 'shopping hungry' when you made those decisions? Can you now appreciate the impact of those decisions on the business, on the teams, or on you personally?

ii. Understanding before being understood
The humility to speak last

It is very easy for leaders (and the default option for some) to think they need to be seen as an all-powerful, all-knowing demigod. However, this behaviour does not serve them and does not create reciprocal relationships across their business.

This leadership style can be appropriate in certain situations (crisis management and times of uncertainty perhaps), but generally is ineffective. A wise, confident leader does not desire to be the most knowledgeable person in the room, or the one that always speaks first; in fact, the opposite is true. To have a room full of people who are well informed on specific subjects and listening to them before you speak is the ideal state. This will give you a chance to learn and, if necessary, shift your position if required before you speak. As any good negotiator knows, getting the other person to state their intention or name their price first is the desirable position to operate from. This puts you on the front foot.

As your company grows in both size and complexity, you can't be the fountain of all knowledge as there is just too much to know. When this happens, understanding what others are seeing, believing and advocating becomes a desirable attribute to acquire and embed into your leadership style.

Across all your key stakeholder relationships, understanding the other party's point of view first, and considering what they need from the relationship, will give you the knowledge and opportunity to create win/win scenarios.

The best and most enduring relationships are where both parties are crystal clear on the expectations of the other. In line with Stephen Covey's principle of understanding before being understood (see Chapter 4), how can stakeholders deliver on expectations if they do not understand what is expected from them?

iii. Rigorous onboarding process
Filter hard and filter early!

In a rapidly expanding company, there is sometimes the temptation to onboard stakeholders too quickly to meet demand. Whether we are referring to employees, customers or suppliers, there can be a dilution of the onboarding process to speed progress. This can work short term, but beyond this is ineffective in finding the correct people.

High performing teams in industry or in the forces, such as the Navy Seals or Royal Marines, have a rigorous onboarding process. They recognise their reputation and future outcomes depend upon this. By setting an initial high barrier to overcome, this separates the suitable from the unsuitable applicants. This means the later, more time-consuming parts of the on-boarding funnel are not wasted on unlikely candidates. Filter hard and filter early is the mantra of these organisations.

Most adolescent companies will create ideal customer personas, but in my experience, very few expand the same rigour to onboarding employees and suppliers. This seems contradictory as businesses probably expect to work with employees and suppliers for at least as long, if not longer than customers.

Rigorous onboarding processes also have the advantage of strengthening the perception of your organisation to those trying to work with or for it. The fact that you're detailed and comprehensive in this first interaction demonstrates to the potential stakeholder that you have standards, you're organised and you know what you want. These things increase your desirability, as it's human nature to be attracted to something potentially unattainable. Additionally, those that survive the process will feel that this relationship is worth investing in, given the effort they have put in to work with or for you. Keep the entry barriers high and you will end up with more of the right quality of stakeholders around you – a win/win situation.

2. Objective detachment
Are you balancing the expectations of your different stakeholders?

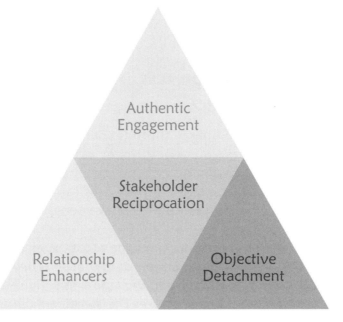

Another critical consideration alongside developing the quality of each individual interaction is whether you are achieving the optimal balance across your relationships. Are you favouring one or more relationship to the determinant of the others? As the ultimate leader within your organisation, the ideal position for you to take is a slightly detached vantage point, so you can objectively assess your balancing act.

Finance and profit distribution are the most obvious, and emotionally sensitive, elements that you need to balance, but equally important is how you allocate your time. Too many CEOs that I have encountered over-focus on the relationship with their customers and prioritise this to the detriment of the other three main stakeholder groups. This is one of the adolescent company behaviour traits that the CEO needs to transition from, as it is neither healthy nor sustainable as the company scales. If you are going to fully develop the other key (as well as new) stakeholder relationships, you need to trust that other people in the company can handle some of these relationships. One of the best ways to achieve this balance is to ensure your diary allocates a set amount of time each month to spend with employees, partners and shareholders. This should be ideally away from your main office, so that you can spend quality time with each group and ensure they feel important. Having a structured diary (with a degree of flexible time built in) is a prerequisite for being an intentional, strategically focused leader, as opposed to a reactive, operationally focused one.

Specifically there are three recommended attributes that underpin the ability to practice *objective detachment*:

i. 'owner mentality' employees

ii. customers as brand ambassadors

iii. partnerships rather than suppliers

i. 'Owner mentality' employees
Do they see what you see?

For an autonomous company to be created from your current dependency-based organisation you need more people to have an 'owner's mentality.' If employees possess this, they will be more accountable and more considerate of outcomes. You need them to be not only contractually and financially connected to the business, but more importantly to have a strong degree of emotional connection. They need to care more than they did before, to be prepared to go beyond what is technically required, and to strive to be better each day.

For most adolescent businesses, the overriding company culture is one of delegated responsibility; by this I mean there are people across the business that have been given responsibility for a certain aspect or function. This culture works to a certain point, as you have people around you to take care of some of your previous responsibilities. However, this culture is more about maintaining the status quo than creating something remarkable. A responsibility culture is perfectly suited to a government organisation or the armed forces, where processes are carried out routinely and identically – no ambiguity, no excuses and no surprises. The downside of a responsibility-based culture is that the ultimate accountability still sits with one or two people at the top of the organisation who need to sanction, approve or sign off the majority of decisions. This is the traditional, hierarchical, pyramid-shaped organisational structure that is standard in most businesses and organisations. Efficiency is championed above effectiveness in this culture.

In contrast, an accountability culture is based on the outcomes, results and implications. Therefore it is naturally more open, inquisitive and boundary pushing than a responsibility culture. It is focused on ownership of decisions and the achievement of objectives and goals. An accountability culture generates an 'owner's mentality' across the employees, where innovation is championed and mistakes are allowed. In this culture, employees have the opportunity to gain an exponential return (in terms of financial reward, promotions and development) if they achieve or go beyond the agreed outcomes and targets.

Where responsibility allows individuals to hide within a traditional structure, accountability focuses attention across the business, allowing the stars to shine wherever they sit within the organisation. A much more fluid organisational structure is present in a company built on an accountability culture.

Of the actions being recommended in this book, I believe this is one of the tougher ones to implement. It requires a significant change for most leaders from the way they currently run their business, which in most cases could be categorised as a 'control and command' mentality. This is where they sign off 99 per cent of the decisions made, and a high percentage of the workforce report directly to them. This should be replaced by a company culture with the twin elements of 'engage and empower' embedded.

Trust your workforce to deliver the desired outcomes once you have set the parameters and the end goal. Your responsibility is to create the structure and allocate enough resources, but then leave your engaged and empowered employees with the agency to perform. Yes, you put benchmarks in place to track progress. Yes, you set up a reporting structure to stay informed. Yes, you graduate the way you introduce this change. However, changes must be made to mature from a 'control and command' mentality. This may feel uncomfortable for a while, but it will be worth it for the freedom you will feel and the healthy culture this will stimulate in your business.

ii. Customers as your brand ambassadors
Raving fans *needed!*

Once upon a time, between the 1960s the 2000s, when advertisers were admirable figures and nobody knew about 'fake news', life was easy for companies. Generally their customers believed what they were told. In this golden age for advertisers, it was a relatively simple process to onboard new customers. All you needed to have was a catchy strapline and a pile of money to buy advertising space. Back then, the winners were the companies that could command the most advertising space irrespective of whether they truly offered consumers a better product or service. Simply, we the consumer trusted the companies that sold to us. All this has changed. This is partly due to the Internet, which gives us the ability to research, and also due to the adoption of a more cynical (some would say less naïve) attitude taken by consumers.

Customers now want evidence and not just data before they make a purchase, they also want to know you are a 'good' company with a purpose, and most significantly they want to hear this information not from you, but from your existing customers. We trust our fellow consumers more than the 'faceless' businesses. Testimonials, case studies and recommendations are the new gold all companies should be looking to mine as this is what customers value most when deciding where to spend.

This shift means it's not enough to have a loyal fan base of passive, regular customers; you now need *raving fans* who are happy to share their experiences. This is so important because more and more purchase decisions take place before a potential customer is even known to the company they may be purchasing from. These decisions are based on testimonials, recommendations and feedback about your company. Current statistics show that in some industries up to 70 per cent of the purchase decision is made before potential customers make themselves known to the organisation. Consumers choose to interact with their counterparts, recommendation sites and influencers before they interact with the company. Therefore you need to be influencing that period before you know them, which is why *raving fans* and influencers must be harnessed.

If you merely meet preset expectations, you will have a satisfied customer, but they are very unlikely to promote your business to others unless you ask them for their opinion. However, if you exceed expectations, you will have created a delighted customer who will be singing your praises without prompting. This means that you need processes and systems for identifying your *raving fans* and, once identified, give them the equivalent of a megaphone so that their delight is communicated widely.

Having a process like Net Promoter Score (NPS) to identify who sits in each customer segment (promoters, passives and detractors) is important. You need to be able to neutralise (or ideally convert) your detractors. You need to have a way of converting passives into promoters. You should create ways for promoters to reach the maximum audience, and become embedded as part of your marketing strategy.

In all likelihood, the marketing strategy and tactics that you have employed to get you to this point won't be enough to take you to the next level. *Raving fans* reduce your required marketing spend, and the more you have, the more savings you make. This in turn means your profits increase, as your acquisitions cost per new customer reduces. In the final element of reciprocal relationships, I will be suggesting ways you can go about this by focusing on outcome-based rewards.

iii. Partners rather than suppliers
Transactional or transformational?

For some companies, the quality of their suppliers is the key factor in their ability to deliver a service to their customers. What I find strange is even with companies whose profits and performances are so dependent on their suppliers, there is still a tendency not to value these relationships the way they should.

There is still a prevailing mindset, which is typified by the way supermarkets have treated the numerous farms that supply their produce, the bigger party dictating the terms, payment schedule, etc., and the smaller partner being expected to accept this way of operating as the price for doing business with these companies. While this may work for both parties in the short term, it is unlikely to be sustainable. There is a fundamental imbalance to the relationship, which means when market conditions tighten and margins need to be trimmed, one party will take the hit and lose out. These types of relationships are transactional in their nature with very little trust present, and no emotional buy-in. This means either party will be happy to jump ship, if a potentially better relationship is on offer – no loyalty is present. If you operate with this mentality as your default, you will be building your business from a very unstable base. As a result, you will forever be concerned about the reliability of your suppliers, who in turn have been treated with mistrust.

The desirable alternative is to have a recurring relationship with your suppliers, where they are treated as long-term partners rather than as short-term solutions. You embed a win/win understanding rather than a win/lose contract. This is where all parties are challenged to be the best they can and the outcomes and rewards for both partners are continually reviewed so the optimal balance is achieved.

For an unpredictable adolescent business to transform into a reliable, mature company, solid foundational relationships must be in place that can deliver as expected and when required. To make this happen, carefully review your existing supplier relationships, and make a commitment to upgrade those with the most long-term potential. This upgrade should result in both parties viewing each other as partners rather than participants in a supplier/customer relationship.

3. Relationship enhancers
How do we go deeper?

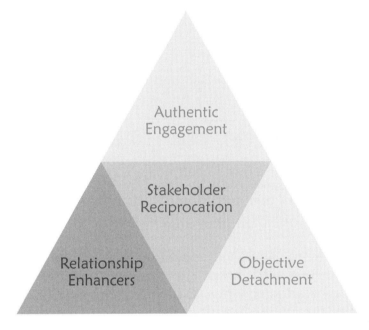

The final element for creating reciprocal relationships with stakeholders is to make sure that you contractually build in both risk and reward to each relationship. For two parties to work optimally together they need to be on an equal footing, which means that there needs to be a similar degree of risk and reward in place for both. If the risk and reward are not similar then the actions, the prioritisation and the intensity that the parties bring to the relationship will be unbalanced.

While the presence of both reward and risk is ideal, it is the presence of an enticing recompense that underpins any engagement. Multiple studies have shown that the removal of pain is the best short-term stimulus, but the gaining of pleasure that has the potential to turn into a longer-term reciprocal relationship. To increase the probability of pleasure, we need to focus on creating and embedding *relationship enhancers*. These are investments which ensure that the other party feels valued and rewarded for continuing the relationship.

All too often relationships are viewed from only a personal perspective and we don't spend enough time considering the other party's point of view. For true reciprocal relationships to be in place, you need to not only appreciate your partner's attitude, but also make sure agreements and understanding are put in place to acknowledge and reward them accordingly.

In order to create an enhanced relationship there are three attributes, which should ideally be present:

i.   WIIFT

ii. milestone acknowledgement

iii. value adding.

i. WIIFT
'Them' is the new 'me'

The 'what's in for me?' mentality doesn't just apply to employees. WIIFM is at the heart of each stakeholder relationship whether it has been verbalised or not.

The ideal scenario companies should be looking to achieve is where there is a contractual and emotional engagement with each stakeholder group. This can be attained when clear expectations are laid out on both sides, and regular communications channels and pre-agreed metrics have been established; these can be used to objectively measure how well the relationship is suiting both parties.

The key question the enlightened business leader needs to ask is 'what's in it for *them*'. For instance, if I were the other party, would I be happy with the return I am receiving from the investment I make to this company (either time or financial or both)? Once you have considered the other party's return on investment, you can then create a true symbiotic relationship that serves both you and them.

Symbiotic relationships are where both parties receive a valued return on their investment, or the time, they spend on the relationship. This return doesn't need to be in the same currency but should be perceived by the receiver as beneficial. It is likely that each stakeholder group will be looking for a different type of return. Therefore the key is ensuring your company can simultaneously offer varying value to different stakeholders, without one group's demands negatively impacting your appeal to other groups.

I appreciate that each company has a limited amount of financial surplus to share between the different stakeholder groups, but this conundrum is not solely money oriented. When employees are asked about what motivates them in the workplace, money and reward often don't make the top three factors. Other motivators may include:

➤ interesting work and projects

➤ feeling appreciated and recognised for their contribution

➤ being empowered to make decisions.

Interestingly, the actual cost of each of these is potentially low; they just require an investment of time from leaders, and the confidence to trust their employees. The same logic applies to other stakeholder groups; look beyond finances to create the optimal reward structure to deepen relationships.

ii. Milestone acknowledgment

Did you remember?

The second key attribute that we should instil into our relationships is ways of recognising and celebrating the milestones. These can operate similarly to wedding anniversaries, as each year comes with a higher-value gift attached to showcase the longevity of the relationship.

Given the amount of data it is possible to hold on to each customer, and the technology at our disposal, it's straightforward to build automated alerts that inform both parties (you and them) when a milestone has been achieved. The type of milestones we might acknowledge may be time based (length of doing business together, years of service, etc.), volume based (certain amount of orders, numbers of transactions between us, etc.), or activity based (reviews given, referrals recommended, etc.). In fact, the type of milestone is far less important: what's significant is recognising something and making a big enough deal out of it.

Making existing customers feel recognised and rewarded for their continued custom is a relatively low investment, compared to the equivalent marketing spend to gain a new one. Customer loyalty and longevity is harder to achieve than ever before because of the increased competition, and relatively low switching costs now in place in most markets. Therefore acknowledging these milestones to recognise existing customers makes logical sense, to retain their business.

It surprises me that service providers often offer better terms to new customers than they do to loyal, existing customers. How many times have you seen mobile phone companies offer a special rate or deal if you switch to their service? What message does this send to existing customers? How are they building long-term relationships with this thinking? Gaining customers is not everything.

The other anomaly I come across regularly is preset increases on the anniversary of the contract, which are well above the rate of inflation, e.g. a five per cent increase each year built in rather than discretionary. This type of contract assumes that the recipient is bound to be satisfied with the service they have received to pay over the odds for the next year. This feels arrogant and wrong to me in the same way that a restaurant which has a ten per cent compulsory service fee on the bill that assumes their service warrants this, even before you have received the service.

Surely, if you want to maintain your existing customers it would be better to fix the fee to the rate which they agreed to pay in year one, or even reduce that fee slightly? There is very little cost associated with renewing an existing client contract, especially when the alternative is to spend marketing and sales investment on 'hunting'.

Introducing loyalty schemes for customers, holiday entitlements schemes biased towards long-serving employees and early settlement discounts for suppliers are all examples of *relationship enhancers* that are simple to implement and have proven successful for companies. Align these incentives to milestones where possible so the other party is motivated to reach them.

iii. Value-adding
Surprise me?

While the first two attributes are overt and should be advertised to the stakeholders in advance, the final attribute needs to be more subjective and covert to be effective. We all have expectations of relationships, based on what was advertised, what was discussed, or what we signed up for. If our expectations are met, the chances are we are going to be satisfied enough to continue that relationship. However, while being satisfied is probably enough to retain our custom, it is unlikely to be enough to turn us into a brand ambassador or raving fan who will independently promote the company. To do this, businesses must create customer delight, and this is only achieved if we receive added value from the relationship.

From a shareholder's perspective a 'value add' is simply something over and above what was expected in the relationship. If there is a relationship contract then it could be quicker delivery, extra discount, or anything better than the agreed terms. If there is no contract in place, it's harder to potentially identify individual stakeholders' expectations. The reward must be appropriate to the stakeholder group you aim to please.

For instance, randomly selecting five customers each month to receive a 'thank you' gift would be one way of achieving customer delight, providing they were satisfied customers in the first place.

From an employee's perspective, it might be as simple as name-checking them in your in-house newsletter or weekly video update, for the service they have given, or maybe rewarding them with an extra perk. The important element is it needs to be subjective (a discretionary choice) and they can't have been expecting it.

For suppliers or partners, it might be an invite to a social event, or tickets to a sports game. You should know your suppliers/partners well enough to identify what they would value as an extra gift or reward. Sending something they have no interest in or won't value has no impact, apart from probably telling them your relationship is undeveloped. The concept of value adds is very simple, but if done well can enhance the way you are perceived as a company by your stakeholders.

Case study

Riverford Organic Farmers

Over the past 30 years, self-confessed veg nerd Guy Singh-Watson has expanded delivering a wheelbarrow of veg to his friends to a nationally acclaimed veg box scheme delivering to over 50,000 customers a week. Part of this success is down to Guy's forward-thinking leadership, as demonstrated by predicting a market for organic veg and having the drive to create a business from his passion. A huge reason for the company's success is that they have engaged, cultivated and maintained reciprocal relationships with each of key stakeholder groups. The support and loyalty of these groups have enabled Riverford to scale the business with greater certainty and confidence.

Riverford's relationships are underpinned by *authentic engagement*. They are upfront about who they are (and who they're not), to ensure that customers and suppliers have similar values and beliefs. They are obsessive about communicating with their customers, creating a trusting relationship. By telling them what's happening on their farms, they can explain what conditions have affected the contents of their veg boxes. Their website has almost as much copy about their 'why', their 'whats' (their values) and their 'how' (their structure and processes) as it does about their products.

I also admire the way they seem to find the ideal balance point between the needs of different stakeholder groups, demonstrating a high degree of *objective detachment*. They are customer focused, but not customer centric, as shown by their statement 'the customer is not always right'. They appreciate that if they pander to their customers too much, other stakeholders, normally suppliers or shareholders, lose out. They demonstrate their objectivity by having a complementary value declaring 'market forces aren't always right'. They work hard balancing different stakeholder needs and never put these ahead of their own values.

By having deeper and longer relationships with their key stakeholders than most companies, Riverford can better understand what the specific stakeholder wants from the relationship. This makes it easier for Riverford to add extra value where and when it is most appreciated, in *relationship enhancers*. During the challenging 2020 summer when the coronavirus pandemic hit the UK, Riverford closed their services to new customers so they could better meet the needs of existing customers as suppliers could not meet increased demands. They did the right thing at the right time to protect all their existing relationships. This commitment was also demonstrated when they moved to an employee-owned trust in 2018, with 74 per cent of the company now being owned by the employees, and then by achieving B-Corp status in 2019. This commits Riverford to considering both the wider population and the planet as additional stakeholders with whom they need to establish a reciprocal relationship.

Guy Singh-Watson is one of the leaders who best embodies my guiding principles. He ensures the company is aligned with its values in a transparent way, while continuing to encourage a degree of vulnerability within business to find better ways of operating. Embedding these principles and establishing reciprocal relationships at the heart of the business has enabled him to create a legacy for the future.

Key takeaways

Summary

Stakeholder reciprocation **and the mantra of** *better before bigger*

You need the detachment and awareness to appreciate that some of your current stakeholders may not be ideal for the next stage of growth; you may need new stakeholders that better fit your aspirations. This may be tough to comprehend and act upon, especially since your success to date has been built around these relationships. This is why detachment is so necessary. This quest for 'better' is about creating the company you aspire to make, rather than pragmatically continuing with a 'that'll do' attitude.

You need to be 100 per cent committed to this process, as you may receive negative reactions unless you successfully articulate the 'why' at the centre of the process. Objectively analyse each relationship one by one, and if you feel it's not satisfactorily productive then you need to upgrade. Making the other party aware of your realisation can sometimes be enough to improve the relationship, but in some cases you will need to be comfortable letting go of long-standing employees or customers. This challenging step is necessary if you are to truly embrace the mantra *better before bigger*.

Stakeholder reciprocation **and the paradox of** *flucture*

You must set standards and expectations that are potentially higher than those currently in place. This will elevate the quality of relationship you have with each stakeholder group. Being clear on what you are offering and what you want to receive in return is vital. By widening this understanding, you will facilitate more concise negotiations with each stakeholder group, clarifying what each party is willing to give and what they want to gain. This will result in productive, ongoing relationships with the correct stakeholders that will last longer than the less ideal agreements you formerly had.

By adding more structure to selecting, onboarding and retaining stakeholders you will reap the rewards by having less churn and higher commitment levels. The old business adage of 'hire slowly, fire quickly' underpins this thinking. Adolescent companies are sometimes shy about identifying unsuitable stakeholders, as they are often 'shopping hungry' to meet short-term targets. Be clear, be confident, and be committed to your values.

Stakeholder reciprocation and the concept of *embracing the plateau*

This is the fun part. In my experience most driven, ambitious leaders can sometimes forget to both celebrate their successes and appreciate what they have achieved to date. They operate on a 'achieve and reset' mode, where once one goal is achieved it is instantly replaced by a new one. This can be tremendously rewarding on one level but can also squeeze out of the processes of recognition, understanding and reflection.

Recognition of achievement, celebrating with stakeholders and giving rewards are fundamental to long-term relationships. Time spent appreciating what has gone well to date (and equally what hasn't), and the factors underpinning success (or failure) are crucial to replicating and building on that success (or turn around that failure).

Adopting an *embracing the plateau* mindset gives you the time and space. This will allow you to evaluate whether you truly have symbiotic relationships in place, which can support your transformational journey.

Reflect and commit

Before moving on to the next chapter, I would encourage you to reflect on whether you currently have quality stakeholder relationships in place to underpin the next phase of growth. Which relationships do you need to upgrade?

1 **Authentic engagement** – do you consider your values enough when making decisions and during onboarding processes, to ensure you are placing these ahead of your short-term needs?

2 **Objective detachment** – do you fully understand your various stakeholders' ambitions and visions, to ensure you are assisting them in achieving these and aligning their needs with yours?

3 **Relationship enhancers** – as a leader, are you good at celebrating successes and do you routinely shine a light on those responsible for achieving their targets and goals?

Now based on those reflections, what are you prepared to commit to change?

I will start...
I will stop...
I will do more...
I will do less...

What's next?
Critical component #4: *Numerical extrapolation*

Now we are hopefully clearer on what good strategy and healthy relationships look like, the next chapter explores how we can use data from across the organisation to monitor the effectiveness of both the strategy and relationships we have in place. I will also explain why organisations should prioritise the presentation of their numbers, and how this enables more informed decisions to be taken.

7. Numerical Extrapolation

Overview

Why is *numerical extrapolation* a core component?

Are you understanding your data or just processing it?

To the uninitiated a set of numbers is just a set of numbers, no more no less. To the more enlightened leader a set of numbers is both a story and a glimpse into the future. Having the right data, presented in a comprehensible format with insightful commentary, enables effective leadership. The story it tells about the past and the explanation it offers for the present helps you to learn and make the changes required to improve future performance. This glimpse into the possible future allows you to understand what your strategic options are and what resources you may need to implement these.

Data extrapolation has become omnipresent; behind every high performing team in any context you will find a well-oiled machine of people and processes to extract and extrapolate data effectively. Without fully understanding what underpins your successes and to what extent each factor has impacted them, how can you be confident of repeating these victories at the next level?

Understanding your data gets more important as your company grows simply because you have more to lose; the stakes have been raised. For this reason, I feel it is a core and not optional component that leaders must be comfortable with before they scale further.

How adolescents work with data
The current challenge

Data overload can drown a growing company if there aren't systems and processes in place to control it. It can cause paralysis (too much information/ too many options), overwhelm (hours consumed working through finance sheets or marketing data), and indecision (we must understand all the numbers before we can make a decision).

As you scale, it's easy for leaders to become overwhelmed and overloaded with the amount of information and reports they must keep abreast of. You end up spending most of your evenings, and some of your weekends, trawling through reports and spreadsheets that have been created to appease your desire to feel in control. This is particularly common in the area of finance, where you can easily lose hours in complex spreadsheets designed by your financial controller or outsourced accountant, which may be designed to demonstrate their mathematical intelligence. You need to make the conscious decision to limit the amount of information you are presented with, if you are going to be able to proactively lead your company as you desire. Your primary role is to lead not to review data.

Look over the emails, reports and updates you have received over the past seven days. How many have actually assisted in your decision-making, and how many have just been background noise that has had little to no impact on your considerations?

How mature companies tend to use their data
The ideal scenario

One change needed, as a company scales, is to switch from a mentality based on functional data (i.e. everything we can measure), to one based on insightful data (i.e. what we actually need to know). Just because we can measure so much doesn't necessarily mean that we should produce reports on all of it. Thinking and behaviour need to be focused on understanding the key, important, relevant numbers in each area of the business to avoid paralysis, overwhelm and time-wasting.

The *inspirational leadership* I am advocating throughout this book comes partly from confidence. Confidence is symptomatic of understanding both the current situation, and importantly, the future scenarios that may occur over the short and medium term. This confidence comes from knowing your numbers and then constructing growth strategies from them. Leaders of mature companies know that bond indicating immediate performance, data is about strategising effectively. To do this, the numbers used should be relevant and specific rather than amorphous.

Considerations

Extrapolation is the process by which we can transform functional data into insightful numbers. Having an on-demand set of updated numbers serves a number of important functions within the business. First, it enables you to keep score, and to know whether you are winning. Sounds simple, but the confidence generated from having this level of insight underpins *inspirational leadership*. Second, a set of insightful numbers helps you to quickly focus attention and resources on problems or potential issues. You can react quicker with greater certainty. Finally, it enables you to accurately assess whether the direction and speed of travel can achieve your short-term goals, medium-term vision and long-term mission. Are we heading in the right direction quickly enough?

There is a massive competitive advantage to be potentially gained here by having a better set of data presented in a more insightful format than your counterparts have. There are so many known unknowns that can exist within a business in relation to the data points and metrics that underpin the visible numbers. If these could be turned into known knowns, it would give a better understanding of why you are currently winning (or losing). Winning without knowing why is not necessarily scalable or repeatable.

When looking to create a better set of numbers and insights, there are three main areas to consider before proceeding.

Alignment to your core commitments
Are we on course?

The main purpose of data is to understand our current situation. Whether it is financial data (bank balances) location data (GPS systems), climate data (temperature), these are all relevant pieces of information from which we can make decisions accordingly. Data is there to serve us. The secondary (and the more insightful) purpose of data is to inform us of the direction of travel for any of the numerous data points we may choose to refer to. Are we better off this month than last month, is it getting warmer or colder, etc.? Data is there to inform. The secondary purpose is of most relevance to leaders, because if the data is extrapolated correctly, it can inform whether you are closer to achieving the goals, vision and mission today than you were yesterday, or last week, or last month.

A relevant and continually updated dashboard is as much an essential tool for a business leader as it is for the pilot of a transatlantic plane. A pilot can instantly tell whether they are going to achieve their mission (to land safely at the agreed destination, on time); does your dashboard give you the same instant response to the same question?

Using data to understand whether you are on track is one part of alignment, the other aspect ensuring your stakeholder agreements are consistent with your core commitments. This will create win/win scenarios along the journey as various milestones are hit. In my experience, aligning company reward and remuneration packages directly to the achievement of the company goals is not done well and often enough in adolescent stage businesses. For some reason, the norm is fixed salary contracts with little risk or reward attached; this potentially means that the employee can win (receive their full salary) even if the company doesn't hit its financial goals. The alternative is to make sure that a proportion of each remuneration package is performance related, to align employees' motivation more closely with the achievement of the company targets and goals. In the same way, supplier contracts should ideally have incentives in place if they perform above the agreed level, and penalties if they fall below. This again should make sure their performance is more closely aligned with achieving agreed milestones.

The better you can align any financial contracts with stakeholders to your core commitments, the greater the probability you are likely to achieve them, as all the stakeholders will be working together.

Enough transparency
Who needs to know what?

By making important numbers visible to different layers of the organisation, you are sharing the responsibility attached to each number. Yes, you, and your most senior financial person, are still accountable for the ultimate financial performance of the business, but by doing this you are encouraging others to take some of the responsibility and, where possible, decision-making.

A classic, and perhaps extreme, example of this transparency is the visionary CEO Ricardo Semler. He went as far as allowing his employees to decide on the appropriate compensation levels across his manufacturing business in Brazil. Semler spent time in advance making sure the employees understood the accounts and the overall company goals, but then gave them the ultimate responsibility for setting the targets and corresponding compensation levels. What was interesting is that the levels the employees set their remuneration at were generally equal to or even lower than what the CEO would have set for them. Therefore if you give enough transparency (and education) then people will probably come to a similar conclusion as you would have reached with the same information.

Now you might not feel comfortable working to this level, but I would encourage you to think about what impact this could have on the company if your employees know more about the financial and business performance. The more business understanding and acumen there is across employees, then the greater probability of sound commercial decisions being made. If you treat your employees as intelligent individuals, the chances are they will act that way.

This logic applies to all business numbers, not just the financial figures. Employees will start to make a connection between their actions and the outcomes they are seeing, enabling them to work out what to do more of and what to do less of to reach the desired goal.

If you currently keep your cards and the numbers close to your chest, then I would not suggest suddenly becoming transparent without any warning, as this may just freak people out. Instead, look at it as a medium-term project, where each month you start to share more important information with a wider number of employees, to a point that makes sense to you. Trust that you have the right stakeholders in place and see what happens when you're more transparent.

Financial vulnerability
Getting comfortable being uncomfortable!

To move from the status quo to a new way of operating in any area of your business always relies to a degree on a 'leap of faith', which is where the vulnerability kicks in. How big a leap you need to make will depend on how prepared you are (have you put the groundwork in before you make the change?), and also how large a gap there is between where you currently are and where you need to be.

Financial vulnerability is not actually about risking finance and making optimistic investments, it refers to openness about how well the company performance. I suggest that before you can move to a new, ideal relationship with your business, you will need to get comfortable with more people knowing the numbers – getting comfortable being uncomfortable.

To encourage you to make this leap, I want to highlight the risks associated with staying with the operational status quo.

First, the finance department will become either too bloated or a bottleneck. You will need to keep adding staff if you depend on them to sign off and monitor every financial decision that has to be made, and this may lead to it becoming too bloated. A bottleneck may occur if you don't either increase the team size or devolve some of the financial decision-making. Neither outcome is desirable and the way to avoid them is to make understanding finances a wider responsibility.

Second, the status quo means that you are not developing the financial skill sets within your senior leadership team and management in the way you could be. You are looking to develop leaders that, in the future, can run the business for you, and a degree of financial acumen is an essential leadership skill in a commercial business. You risk losing good leaders if you don't challenge them to take on more financial responsibility.

Third, if you don't devolve the financial decision-making, and increase the amount of financial awareness across the company, you are pinning a lot of pressure on the finance team to control areas of the business they may have very little understanding and/or influence. This will result in an overly conservative culture which will look to eliminate any risk. Ideally, we always need a healthy balance between risk and reward, so having other leaders and team members who can challenge the financial numbers and decisions will result in a healthier, more efficient business culture.

Yes, there are risks here, but if this is implemented as a planned roll-out programme, and you spend enough time explaining the why, the whats and the hows as you proceed, you will reduce the amount of risk considerably.

Essential elements & desirable attributes

Now that we have looked at the bigger 'why' alongside the effective communication of data across a company, I want to look more specifically at the ingredients needed to make these changes, to facilitate growth.

1. Contextual analysis
Is your data being delivered with enough reference points to inform decision-making?

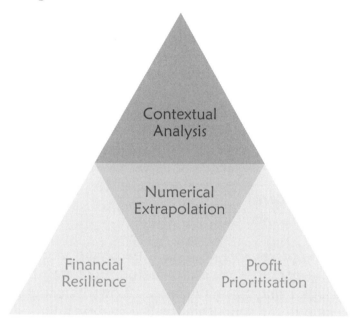

Back in the 1980s there was a programme on TV in the UK called *Think of a Number*, presented by Johnny Ball. What seemed remarkable was his ability to make something as potentially mundane as numbers come to life in an engaging way. At the time, and being of school age, my relationship with numbers was confined to maths lessons which meant algebra, equations, etc. I considered these very dry topics and not things I could relate to in a meaningful way. I think financial information within most companies could do with a 'Johnny Ball makeover' to make it come alive, to engage an audience outside of the finance department. Like all departments, finance has its own terms and abbreviations, and these can end up alienating an outsider. It can feel like an exclusive club, which you are not entitled to enter or comment on, unless this behaviour is checked. In essence, it comes down to a willingness and desire to look at numbers differently.

There is a need for compliance around the way numbers are reported to external agencies, but apart from that, leaders sometimes forget that internally they get to dictate to whom and how they are presented. Too many leaders accept the default version offered by the finance team, who have been taught to present them in a standard format.

If one of the functions of the numbers is to enable more informed decision-making, not only the format but contextualising the financial information is also critical to ensure there is a real understanding of their meaning.

If you are going to make the financial information both more accessible to a wider audience and more insightful, three attributes must be present to provide a relevant framework and to tell the required story:

i.   variances to inform

ii. ratios to predict

iii. performance metrics to empower.

i. Variances to inform
Give me a comparative, please

The first attribute of variance analysis is becoming more commonplace as most software packages have this feature built into their reporting functions. The logic being that a number on its own is neither good nor bad but needs to be put into some comparative context before any meaning can be drawn. Therefore your financial reports should always show a comparative to the actual number you are reporting, and then a variance from this comparative number, i.e. what was the same number last month, last quarter, or last year? And consequently, what is the variance between the current number and the previous one? Or alternatively, a comparative to what you had expected or budgeted for works in the same way.

Making sure there is a variance figure present in your financial reports allows everyone who reads or reviews the financials to come to the discussion from the same starting point. If results are contextualised straight away then you can spend more time discussing the reasons for the performance and the implications for the future, which is a far more beneficial use of time.

Once you have a variance in place, the next step is to make sure you assess the number by categorising it; this will determine the acceptability of this variance. For instance, if your turnover is tracking five per cent behind the same month last year this might be acceptable, as that level of variance could just be down to a localised factor, such as a change in personnel, or more adverse weather impacting customers visiting your stores, etc. Therefore one-off, short-term factors. In contrast, a variance of, say, 25 per cent behind the same period would be far more concerning. This would require deeper analysis to understand what has changed and what actions should be taken to reverse this trend. This process is commonly known as 'ragging', where you apply a red, amber or green rating depending on the percentage variance and your preset tolerance targets. You set the targets and specify in advance what is acceptable performance across your various numbers and metrics. This type of process simplifies the data into a standard format, which is easily understood by anyone viewing the data.

By working off variances rather than raw data, you have to spend very little time on subjectively discussing and agreeing with others whether the number is good or bad. Instead, you can spend much more time focusing on solutions and improvements. In short, variances inform in a way that pure numbers don't.

ii. Ratios to predict
Where are we under/overperforming?

The second type of attribute that assists with extrapolated data, making it more accessible, is ratios. Ratios are used to show the relationship between two figures so that more understanding can be gleaned from the pure data. For instance, your net profit percentage (net profit divided by turnover) is one of the simplest ratios for benchmarking your business against direct competitors in the same industry. A company with a higher net profit percentage is judged as running more efficiently than one with a lower percentage. In the same way, if you look at gross profit percentage generated per project, it will give you clarity of who your most effective project managers are, or which types of projects deliver a higher return on investment.

There are commonly four sets of financial ratios that you should understand and embed into your business reporting to enable accurate assessment of how well your organisation is currently operating. These are the same ratios that external investors use to assess the value of a company.

1 **Liquidity ratios** demonstrate a company's ability to pay its short-term debts and liabilities. If these are positive and in acceptable parameters, it means your business model is fundamentally sound and you can sleep well each night.

2 **Activity ratios** demonstrate how efficiently the business operates, and how well it uses its resources to generate sales and profit. These are important to perfect before you get too much bigger, as they're all about eliminating waste and being lean. As companies grow, these are crucial to observe to make sure you are getting *better and not just bigger.*

3 **Leverage ratios** demonstrate the ability to pay long-term debt and the consequential risk the company faces. These underpin your ability to grow rapidly, and if you are too highly geared it will make future growth a greater risk, unless you can start to reduce these ratios to acceptable levels.

4 **Performance (or profit) ratios** demonstrate the ability to generate a return for your shareholders. You may be one of the main shareholders in the business, so these are important to make sure you get a return today and not just reinvesting continually for some mythical future date when profitability arrives. A solid business should have a good level of profit generated each year, to underpin future growth and to reduce the amount of external investment needed to fund this.

A good set of financial reports will contain a range of relevant ratios and trend lines along with the financial data, so performance can be judged more objectively, and negative trends can be identified early and rectified.

For the majority of these ratios, it is very easy to find both industry-specific and more generic benchmarks to assess your company against, so a comparative position on each should be established. Knowing your ratios will either give you the confidence to grow your company as planned or it may give you a reality check, highlighting areas that require work before further growth can occur.

iii. Performance metrics to empower
What does good look like?

The final attribute of a well-presented set of financial reports is the inclusion of some non-financial metrics. This is so that the relationship between the financial decisions, policies and overall business performance can be identified and measured. For instance, Net Promoter Score is becoming a widely accepted metric for assessing customer satisfaction ratings, which can be linked to both retention levels and average spend per customer. If you have a high NPS you can confidently predict retention levels staying the same or improving. It gives greater validity to any financial projections you make around the future income generated from customers. Similarly, if you make an investment in your marketing or website, you need to put the monetary cost in the context of the higher number of enquires you will receive, or the increased visitors to your website. These non-financial metrics are just as important, as they demonstrate the impact of the financial decisions and show causality, enabling you and your senior leadership team to make more informed commercial moves.

Metrics are also used widely to monitor and reward both individual and team performances in mature companies. Internal scoreboards or dashboards illustrating departmental metrics are now becoming commonplace. These dashboards keep the company agile, facilitating quick response to numbers; without them, decision-making could become far more subjective and erratic.

These types of performance metrics also enable leaders to empower those they lead by giving them very precise targets to meet across all aspects of the duties they perform. An added bonus of this approach is that it facilitates the introduction of performance-related pay and/or bonuses, aligning individual performances more closely with the overall business goals. Less time needs to be invested in monitoring behaviours if you have processes in place for rewarding desirable outcomes. In essence, metrics allow you to treat your employees as your peers and work alongside them to achieve mutually beneficial outcomes.

2. Profit prioritisation
Sanity before vanity

There is an old business adage that suggests turnover equates to vanity and profit equates to sanity, which I feel sums up the reality of running a business well. However, I am still amazed by the number of business leaders who will summarise their business around their turnover or numbers of employees, rather than speaking about their net profit, net profit percentage or EBITDA (earnings before interest tax, depreciation and amortisation – a standard metric used to measure like-for-like performance across different time periods in the same company or across different companies).

We can get seduced very easily by the size of a business and forget that its purpose is to generate a return for its shareholders (unless it's a not-for-profit or charity). Recent history has demonstrated that just because your company is big, or has been around for a number of years, this is no indication of whether it is scalable or sustainable. There have been numerous liquidations of well-established brands which seemingly disappeared overnight. They ran out of cash because their profits were too low to sustain their borrowings or overhead commitments. The leaders of these businesses either ignored the warning signs, or were oblivious to them, and in the end their lack of profitability caught up with them.

Profitability gives you strategic options, as well as sanity. It also demonstrates to the outside world that you possess commercial acumen, and you can manage finance to generate a return. This is a desirable trait valued by commercial partners and potential investors.

My advice to you is, if you are not already doing so, forget size and become obsessed with profit. Profit is a far more reliable indicator of growth ability, and it will underpin both future scalability and saleability of your business.

So if step one is prioritising profit over turnover, step two is setting up your profit and loss reports. From these you can instantly see the percentage of profits being achieved across the main, commonly measured profits. Step three is having a clear goal and strategy for how you are going to improve or at least maintain each of the previous steps.

Now, let's look specifically at the three attributes that underpin the most common types of profit measured:

i.   maximising gross profit

ii. controlling the operating profit percentage

iii. net profit conundrum.

i. Maximising gross profit
Do you have a proactive or reactive pricing strategy?

The first focus should be on achieving a healthy level of genuine gross profit (that is the income minus the direct cost of goods sold). I say genuine, because too many businesses falsely increase this figure (and the gross profit percentage) by excluding all direct costs associated with the delivery or purchase of the goods and services sold. Obviously without a healthy gross profit percentage, it is very difficult to generate a healthy EBITDA at the bottom of your profit and loss, so a continual focus on the gross profit margin is required. This means two things: one, constantly reviewing the pricing strategy to make sure you are maximising the sales price, and simultaneously, two, a constant review of the cost of goods (both the purchase and delivery costs) to ensure these are minimised. A good pricing strategy needs to be both flexible and dynamic to stay competitive but should also align with your brand positioning. Other businesses will have different cost bases and varying business strategies. Therefore there is a real danger that if your pricing strategy is dictated by your competitors' prices, you may end up selling ineffectively and unaligned with your business model, thus making very little gross profit.

Of course, it is very tempting to price-match your direct competitors whenever possible, but this is only advisable if you have a lower cost base or lower purchasing price. These factors may help you generate higher profit margins than your competitors, but without these price-matching can be very risky.

Lidl and Aldi can afford to price-match or lower their prices below the traditional UK supermarkets as they buy cheaper products (less well-known brands), and have lower staffing levels, giving them a lower operating margin and cost base.

Yes, you need to win business and market share, but in the medium term you can only do this at a price that makes you money. The number of customers you have is a relevant and important statistic, but the money you make per customer is a more vital one.

This is where businesses can fall into the trap of trying to maximise turnover at the expense of gross profit margin. The gross profit margin needs to be maintained and should be improved as you scale up, because your buying power will become greater with the higher volumes you purchase, and your delivery costs should reduce due to economies of scale. Understand what gross profit percentage you need, then prioritise that figure over your turnover. This is crucial to create a healthy and sustainable EBITDA.

ii. Controlling the operating profit percentage
Keeping hold of the reigns is imperative

The next focus needs to be on the operating profit. There are a few schools of thought about what should be included in the costs section here. My preference is for reflecting the sales and marketing costs, as these are subjective and can be flexed and varied, depending on the requirements and strategy of the business – unlike the overheads/fixed costs, which as the name implies are going to be similar, whatever the requirements and strategy you put in place. How much money you invest in marketing and selling your product is a monthly decision at least, and if you are selling online it's probably daily. Therefore I think it gives you a false picture if you combine these costs with general overheads like rent and rates, etc., which you cannot vary month to month, let alone daily. What we are trying to demonstrate with the operating profit percentage is how efficient the business is at acquiring new customers and selling to existing customers.

Too many businesses add extra cost in here without fully understanding the level of sales needed to justify that investment. I will go through this in more detail when we discuss the next attribute (investment strategy), but it is an important consideration, and unless you are isolating these costs in your profit and loss statement, one which is hard to track. The operating profit will also illustrate how well you are selling to existing customers, and how many repeat orders you get. This means you don't need to fixate on generating new customers to maintain turnover.

As we have already discussed, selling to existing customers is far cheaper, and therefore more profitable, than selling to new ones. So if you have a good strategy for retaining, upselling and referral generation, this will be reflected in the percentage of your turnover that should invest in sales and marketing. During the adolescent phase, the amount you invest in sales and marketing will almost certainly increase, but the percentage of the turnover this figure represents should reduce. This should be seen if your retention strategy is working effectively and you are maximising existing relationships.

iii. Net profit conundrum
Harvest or reinvest?

Finally we look at net profit (or EBITDA). This will dictate how quickly you can continue growing your business organically without the need to seek any external investment. If you are generating healthy net profits, after all your overheads and tax have been paid, then you will have 'surplus' cash to reinvest in future growth. You will also have enough profit to harvest to satisfy the expectations of your shareholders. A good net profit percentage gives you options but can only be achieved if you prioritise the first two types of profit successfully.

Net profit is a lag metric, whereas gross and operating profits are lead metrics, i.e. ones you can impact more easily. If you are looking to lose weight, calories consumed and calories burnt are lead indicators, and your body weight at the end of the week is a lag indicator. This is only going to be positive if the first two indicators are positive.

There are a number of ways to manage the conundrum of net profits. Some businesses will set advance percentages for allocation, irrespective of the actual figure achieved, e.g. 50 per cent goes to the shareholders in the form of dividends, 20 per cent going to the leadership team as performance bonuses, and 30 per cent stays in the company to fuel future growth. An alternative way is to allocate amounts to different functions, i.e. the first £X,000s stay in the business, the next £Y,000s go back to the shareholders, and the surplus is used for bonuses and rewards. There is no right or wrong approach here, but it is better if you have preset and shared ways of distributing profits so you can manage expectations from the outset. By having a clearly articulated strategy for the distribution of profits, all stakeholders can understand the impact of strategic decisions made during the year on their potential return.

The way you establish the distribution of net profits needs to account for a number of factors, including:

➤ the ambition of your future growth plans and the funding required

➤ whether you have alternate sources of finances available to partially, or fully, fund future growth

➤ whether you are confident that the current level of profitability can be maintained or increased over the next financial period

➤ whether it is a core component of your remuneration packages

➤ the overall market and economic conditions.

In conclusion, the decision around how much of your net profits to harvest and how much to reinvest is not straightforward, and there are multiple factors to consider. Just make sure you are aligned to your values, you are transparent with those that need to know, and that you are vulnerable enough to share the burden.

3. Financial resilience
Do we have strong enough foundations in place?

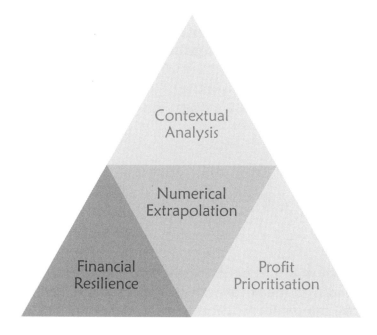

For leaders to confidently implement their strategic plans they need to be sure that they have the required amount of *financial resilience* in place to cope with potential future scenarios. The word financial can be interchanged here with business, as the two go hand in hand. A business cannot be deemed resilient if it does not possess the appropriate financial reserves to call upon when required.

Lack of finance is not only the number one reason businesses fail, but also a large contributory factor to why most never make the transformation from adolescence to maturity. As I have already advocated, contextualising your figures and prioritising profit percentages are two pieces of the jigsaw that will improve resilience. The missing piece is having the organisational capability, and the leadership curiosity, to spend time visualising what the future could look like. Without a clear picture of the future possibilities, it is impossible to make the required financial plans. More insightful reporting, and intensifying the focus on profit, are leadership activities concerned with the here and now, and are relatively easy to implement. The challenge of instilling the third element of *financial resilience* is because it is an activity which pushes you to conceive what *may* happen. This, of course, is more complex than perceiving the past and present.

Building *financial resilience* is not so much about turning known unknowns into known knowns, as that is will only improve your insight to a limited degree. It is about discovering unknown unknowns so that they become known unknowns. Identifying the unknown unknowns is hugely important because it can give you the chance to assess future threats and opportunities, making the next steps seem far less intimidating.

Building *financial resilience* can be achieved by focusing on these specific attributes:

i. 'what if' scenarios

ii. balancing lead and lag metrics

iii. multiple perspectives.

i. What if…?
How prepared are we for future opportunities or threats?

One opportunity that has been created by the increased availability of data, combined with the advancement in software, is the ability for even relatively small companies to spend time on scenario-planning. Only a few years ago most leaders had to rely solely on lag data to try and predict future performance. This was tricky as there were so many unknown variables to consider. This predictive reporting function in modern software allows leadership teams to spend time working through 'what if' scenarios before deciding on a specific course of action. It also allows leaders to drill down to the key drivers and factors that impact overall performance. This provides the opportunity to scenario-plan across all areas of your business, and to work out the impact of any changes in the key drivers on the overall business performance.

As the senior leadership team begin to delegate accountability for most of the operational decisions, this should free up more time for strategic thinking. Part of this thinking time should ideally be allocated to scenario-planning so that the business is better equipped to deal with changes. By having multiple scenarios in play once, you can easily predict the future financial impact of each, thus allowing you to build the required *financial resilience* to cope with all of the potential outcomes. The further you can project into the future, the greater the amount of *financial resilience* you can create.

Most adolescent businesses don't prioritise scenario planning, as it does not seem urgent and, as outlined in the Eisenhower Decision-Making Matrix earlier, it's very easy to spend time on urgent tasks rather than important ones. If you don't give yourself and your leadership team the time and space to pursue this exercise well, you will become a reactive company rather than a proactive one. Scenario-planning facilitates considered action, as opposed to a reaction, which is instantaneous. The former is calculated and delivered with a fair degree of certainty; the latter is instinctive and implemented with a high degree of hope involved.

ii. Balancing lead and lag indicators
Are we looking at the right numbers?

Too many leaders over-focus their attention on the obvious lag indicators, monitoring what has already happened, e.g. the numbers on a profit and loss statement. Not enough priority is given to understanding more critical lead indicators which will dictate future performance, e.g. the number of proposals the sales team have sent out this week.

This shift from considering lag to lead indicators needs to be applied across all areas of your business if you are going to improve the quality of your scenario-planning. This will allow you to better perceive how financially exposed you could be in different scenarios. It is no longer acceptable not to have real-time dashboards across your business, giving your decision-makers the quality and immediacy of data they need to inform their choices. For example, if the only numbers coming out of the finance department are your 'historically focused' profit and loss, cash flow forecast and monthly balance sheet, the business is not getting the quality of data it needs. The sales team need to know whether their gross profit probability percentage is increasing or decreasing with each sale made. The operations department must know whether the cost of every widget produced is trending up or down. The marketing department needs to know whether the marketing spend as a percentage of gross profit is within the target range. All of these pieces of lead data should ideally be instantly visible, or at the very least accessible on demand.

iii. Multiple perspectives
Are you using a single or varifocal lens?

To build the optimal amount of *financial resilience* into your organisation, the final attribute needed is multiple perspectives, i.e. seeing the current and future scenarios through different lenses. None of us are truly impartial on how we view either a set of data or a potential scenario, as we all have previous experiences and preset expectations that impact our judgement. We are all guilty of seeing what we want to see to some extent. While objectivity is an ideal trait to possess, we have to accept that it's almost impossible to be 100 per cent detached. The best way to counteract this bias is to bring others on board who will see things differently. The convergence of these different views will give you a balanced and robust overall perspective on any specific data or scenario.

One of the structural differences between an adolescent and mature company is the latter normally has a board of directors in place to bring multiple viewpoints and a high level of challenge to the leadership team. Ideally, the board is made up of individuals with different expertise and experiences – varying lenses.

Having the humility and awareness to ask for other opinions that may challenge your own or those of your leadership team is the attribute all good leaders possess. Critical friends and external sounding boards may seem like an unnecessary luxury when you are an adolescent stage company. However, they will provide you with an extra layer of insight and enhanced accountability that will ensure your strategy and financial plans are resilient. While this extra layer of scrutiny may seem both time consuming and not necessarily desirable, the benefits far outweigh the costs and time involved. If you choose your critical friends wisely, you will benefit from enhanced confidence in your strategy, as it has been rigorously challenged before implementation. As your business scales, the situations it faces will become more complex; therefore this diversity of perspective is essential.

Ideal extrapolation results in your numbers and scenarios being scrutinised more thoroughly. This additional attention will enable you to see further, wider and with greater clarity, therefore helping you to lead with greater certainty.

Case study

Billy Beane – Oakland As

Every so often a leader comes along that revolutionises the way a market, or in this case a sport, operates. Billy Beane was such a leader who, in the early 2000s, transformed the way baseball teams operated and more specifically how they valued and recruited players.

Baseball, like many sports, creates a lot of data; everything within the game can be measured and analysed. Every team and player is continually evaluated by the numbers they produce. It is a statistic heavy, and some would say, obsessive sport. Despite all the available data, it wasn't until Beane's approach that the subjective recruitment of players was revolutionised. Previously, teams relied on experienced scouts (often former players) to recommend who should be bought and sold in the annual draft. The successful acquisitions and adjustments a team makes during the draft process will have a significant effect on their performance during the season.

Beane realised that all scouts were looking for the same attributes in players, such as obvious lag metrics like the number of home runs or the speed of their pitch. Consequently, a small team like Oakland with a lower budget could not compete for the obvious star players. Beane considered things differently, realising there was another set of player data and attributes which was being ignored, but potentially was equally valuable. This data was based around lead metrics, such as how many bases they could steal, or how little they were caught or struck out. These attributes demonstrated their willingness to play a secondary role when required, rather than stealing the limelight. Beane realised that some players were undervalued because the scouting system was based on subjectivity and headline lag metrics. He radically employed a data analyst, without experience in baseball, to build a model of an ideal team in terms of skill sets and attributes. With this system in place, Beane recruited players that other teams overlooked, staying within his meagre budgets (in baseball terms). However, he managed to produce a series of teams that outperformed expectations, and almost won the baseball Holy Grail, the World Series. The fact that Beane's approach was then adopted and iterated by every team in baseball over the next decade shows the impact and value of his new thinking.

At the heart of Beane's approach was *numerical extrapolation*. The numbers he used to assess players weren't new, as they were available to everyone, but other teams did not realise their importance. The first thing he did was to create a new framework to view the data, providing a different context and asking different questions. The data was the same possessed by the other teams, but the *contextual analysis* was unique, resulting in different (strategic) recruitment decisions being made. Within sport there are really two types of profit that need to be considered: financial success and competitive success (games won). What Beane balanced effectively was the importance of both. His *profit prioritisation* was based on ensuring financial investment was only made on players that had a high probability of success on the field. He didn't gamble, he worked the odds and made logical investments. The *financial resilience* of Beane's model was far higher than most of his contemporaries as he purchased undervalued assets (players), and therefore maintained a strong balance sheet throughout. Unlike most of the other general managers, he was obsessed with lead, not lag, indicators; from this he created a very clear model for winning games aligned with his recruitment and investment policy.

Beane was a trailblazer who thought differently and used the available data to draw new conclusions. Using his conceptual originality, he could provide a higher return on investment than expected to his stakeholders, which is the hallmark of an exceptional leader.

Key takeaways
Summary

Numerical extrapolation and the mantra of *better before bigger*

Most businesses don't need more data, what they need is a better process for understanding and extrapolating trends from the data they have. Many lack the skill set to do this effectively, so they may need to invest in a person or outsource this missing element to a specialist company to do this for them.

By using a specialist (either employee or contractor), you are giving this component the importance it warrants and bringing an increased level of objectivity to the way data and numbers are interpreted within your company. Existing leaders and managers all suffer from varying degrees of tunnel vision; they can be guilty of deliberately misinterpreting data to deny worrying trends. For better financial modelling to be put in place and for the strategic focus to be built around profitable growth rather than just growth, there is a need to consider financial and resource efficiency. Better, detached interpretation of your numbers underpins this focus.

Numerical extrapolation and the paradox of *flucture*

In relation to the paradox of *flucture*, most adolescent companies make understanding their data more complicated and time consuming than it needs to be. This is usually because they are not structured enough in the way they report and share numbers. This inconsistency of presentation makes it harder and slower for strategic decisions to be made. Unintentionally, they are making life more difficult for themselves by allowing too much flexibility and individualism in their financial reporting.

Adopt standard company-wide reporting templates, using the same dashboard tool to create consistent departmental and personal dashboards. Ensure that trends above just current performance are highlighted. By doing this, companies can quickly elevate their numerical function to a better and more structured level. There are standard, proven tools for all of these recommendations that will give a high and instant return on investment if they are adopted across the company, and the use of them is made mandatory.

In short what is needed here is more objective (evidence-based) and less subjective (gut feel-based) reporting, so that better-informed decision-making can happen.

Numerical extrapolation **and the** **concept of** *embracing the plateau*

Financial competency is too often seen as a skill set required by the finance department; however, high-performance organisations will have individuals in all departments who possess a high degree of financial acumen. There is a real and present danger that if the finance department are the only ones who really understand the business numbers, they will have too much influence on decision-making. For an effective leadership team to function, each member needs to understand the reports and numbers from other departments. Ideally, if required, they could then present to the rest of the company on any of the departments confidently.

Developing data competency across your leadership and management teams will not only allow them to take more control and make more informed decisions but will also simultaneously free you from having to guide them through the numbers.

One of the specific outcomes of the business transformation programme I recommend is freeing yourself from some of the day-to-day activity so you can spend more time on your wider mission and vision. Improving the financial acumen of those around and below you will allow you to focus time elsewhere with more confidence and conviction, knowing that good financial decisions are being made independent of your direct input.

Reflect and commit

Before moving on to the next chapter, I would encourage you to reflect on whether you have the quality of data and reporting in place to enable you to make accurate, timely and considered decisions. What might currently be missing?

1 **Contextual analysis** – are you demanding enough from those who report into you, or is there room for improvement in relation to both the financial and non-financial data they deliver?

2 **Prioritising profit** – are you clear on what your ideal percentage profit margins are for your three key types of profit, and what specifically impacts these margins?

3 **Scenario-planning** – do you model the impact of changes in your key metrics in your future financial performance?

Now based on those reflections, what are you prepared to commit to change?

I will start...
I will stop...
I will do more...
I will do less...

What's next?
Critical component #5: *Reputational maximisation*

All the critical components we have considered so far are primarily internally focused, which have impact externally, but generally fall directly under the control of the leadership. The next component is different, as it requires you to consider how the organisation is perceived by those outside the company, whom you have less direct control of. *Reputational maximisation* is concerned with how you can effectively influence how your brand and company are perceived.

8. Reputational Maximisation

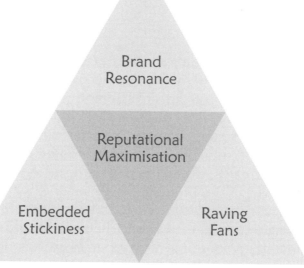

Brand Resonance

Reputational Maximisation

Embedded Stickiness

Raving Fans

Overview

Why is *reputational maximisation* a core component?

Are you paying enough attention to your biggest asset?

Finding potential customers is no longer necessarily the biggest challenge businesses face, as markets grow exponentially, as Internet availability increases and ease of delivery improves every year. The challenge now surrounds gaining sufficient attention from customers. Potential customers are abundant; what's scarce is their attention. We (the customer) tend to give our attention in direct proportion to how much a brand resonates. If we are entertained, educated or excited by a brand, then we pay them more attention. Therefore businesses must have a strategy for maximising the impact their brand has on customers.

Brand presence, positioning and impact are as crucial as the quality of the services and products offered. Just having the best offering is no longer enough to win and retain customers. We are all 'guilty' of purchasing inferior products or services that are either more expensive or lower specification because the company has a brand that resonates more with us than its competitors. Building a brand should be differentiated from other marketing activities because it is so important. Having a strong brand is a selling point that will set companies apart from their competitor. By maximising their reputation through brand identity, businesses can evolve more effectively.

How adolescent companies approach maximising their reputation
The current challenge

The infant and adolescent stages, for most companies, are purely based on a growth focus with a strong emphasis on the need to acquire new customers or sell more products. Investment is made in sales (and sales teams) and marketing activity, but this investment is primarily onboarding new customers. What sometimes gets forgotten during this growth phase is the importance of retaining existing customers, and the additional opportunities that exist within their current customer base. However, there comes a point in the business life cycle curve when it makes much more strategic and financial logic to switch the primary focus from finding and nurturing new customers to a more balanced approach. This balance comes from investing more time and resources on making the best return from existing customers and assets as well as finding new ones.

Too often companies can be guilty of creating better value offers for new customers. It is during this phase where brand development can be forgotten, as marketing activities take priority. An investment in developing the brand will not necessarily give the same instant return that a similar size investment in marketing or sales could make; however, this short-term thinking seriously underplays the importance of the existing customer base.

How mature companies approach maximising their reputation
The ideal scenario

Mature companies appreciate the importance of retention, reselling and referrals from an economic perspective. There are three key understandings that underpin this point:

1 Retaining an existing customer requires a far smaller financial investment than finding a new one. Even accounting for the reduction in acquisition costs created by online marketing, for the majority of businesses, the financial logic works very much in favour of investing in retention ahead of acquisition.

2 Increasing the spend or upselling of existing customers is again an easier and more cost effective than investing the equivalent amount in new customer acquisition. Very few companies have maxed-out their existing relationships.

3 Happy and loyal existing customers can be the central and most cost-effective part of any new customer acquisition strategies that you put in place. It is well known that referrals provide a higher quality potential customer than any other equivalent onboarding channel.

'Sweating your assets' to get the best return is one of the fundamental principles of effective financial strategy. If and when you sell your business, the value of your existing customers and contracts are classified as an intangible asset. Mature companies will have separate budgets and teams purely focused on maximising the return from existing customers and driving the customer lifetime value (CLTV) as high as possible.

Considerations

As businesses scale, they realise that not all income is of equivalent quality. They start to appreciate that *recurring* income (regular income from the same customer) has a higher value and longevity than *re-occurring* (regular income from the same customers but at random intervals); this likewise is better than *transactional* income (one-off sales with no probability of a secondary purchase). Businesses built on transactional income must continually engage new customers and are very exposed to external factors. Whereas organisations built on fixed term and fixed amount recurring contracts have both high predictability and less exposure. They have an almost guaranteed baseline income each month as a starting point.

The type of income stream you can rely on is impacted by the customers' perception of your brand. The more trust and loyalty you have created, the more customers are will likely commit to some form of contracted regular payments. This reliable recurring income stream, if it can be established, gives you strong foundations to build from. It also makes financial projections much easier, which is why it is valued so highly by investors and other lending institutions. However, unless there is required investment in building the brand reputation, as well as the quality of the services and products you offer, it's much harder to get these commitments.

There are three specific considerations I would encourage you to think about, as they directly impact the way you are perceived by existing and potential customers.

Brand is omnipotent
Have you got enough 'brand width' in place?

Before social media was available, when customers generally believed what they were told and asked few questions, there was very little differentiation between the meaning of brand and marketing, from both a customer's and company perspective. Back then marketing was king and there was a very simple equation for companies to work from: the more people that you expose to your brand, the more sales you will generate. Customers weren't really interested in your vision, mission and values; all they wanted was a transactional relationship at the best price. However, as competition has grown, and customers have become savvier about whom they buy from, everything has changed.

Now there is a clear delineation of a company's brand position and its marketing. Customers still want to buy great products and services at the best value, but they also want to buy them from a company whose brand resonates with them, i.e. shares the same values, treats its employees well, does good things with its profits, etc.

Brand has become omnipotent. It is a 24/7, 365-days-a-year focus, to make sure we do nothing to create a negative image of our company. On the flip side, there is continual pressure to create a constantly engaging and relevant brand. In the iconic 1980s film *Wall Street*, the infamous Gordon Gekko lived his life and ran his businesses with some firmly held beliefs, one of which was 'money never sleeps'. I think if the film were remade today, we could easily substitute the word money for brand. 'Brand never sleeps' is one of the modern-day truths that businesses can't afford to ignore.

Your brand is no longer the responsibility of the marketing department, it is a company-wide initiative. There are so many touchpoints that potential and existing customers can now have with your company, both before and while they do business with you. Each touchpoint represents an opportunity to either increase or decrease your reputation. Possessing customers aligned to your brand has gone from being merely desirable to being a 'table stake' to allow you to effectively compete in the market. Sure, if you deliver an amazing brand experience that exceeds expectations, it becomes a differentiator, but in the first instance it is about creating a consistent brand experience that can be constantly delivered.

Having clear brand guidelines, a defined mode of communicating and a standardised company approach to social media are no longer optional extras; these are essential cornerstones if you are going to maximise your brand reputation.

Positioning the paywall
Are we throwing enough breadcrumbs?

Another key consideration is where to position the paywall that separates your free and monetised offerings. What services or products are you prepared to give away as part of your acquisition strategy and what are going to charge for? Due to increased competition, there is pressure on companies to entice new customers with free offers, trial periods, etc. The logic being that once they have had a taster they will come back for more. A good example of an option currently being tried is the online newspapers that coexist alongside their paid-for physical versions. Some newspapers offer a restricted online version for free and ask for a voluntary donation, while others just give a taster before requiring you to subscribe. Each has taken a strategic decision as to where to position its paywall.

Each business has to work through the same strategic decision-making process as there is now an expectation from customers that they should be able to try out or taste something before they commit. It is a fine balancing act because if you give too much ahead of a commitment/payment, you will impact your profit margins. On the other hand, if you give too little, you may negatively impact the numbers willing to try you out. There are a number of factors to consider here:

➤ how established and well respected your brand is – the logic being that newer and less proven brands will have to give more away

➤ how competitive your marketing is – the more competition, the more you will need to entice potential customers

➤ how much gross margin you make per transaction – a higher margin enables you to give more away.

The key is to make sure you have an accurate way of tracking the results of your chosen strategy so you can record both the amounts you are spending to acquire, but also which offers are giving the greatest return on investment. For instance:

➤ If you are selling a piece of software, what is the optimum length of the trial offer period after which it starts to have little or no impact on the conversion rate to the paid version?

➤ If you are selling services, how much free time do you need to invest in a potential client ahead of a paid contract?

It comes down to how and where you want to position your brand, as if you give away too much you could be perceived as a brand with very little intrinsic value. Alternatively, if you give away too little you may alienate potential customers by being too exclusive.

The power of emotions
Are we appealing to the head or the heart?

In the 20th century, marketing and branding were focused primarily on communicating the benefits of the product or service so that potential customers could see why this was better than the competitors' offering. The primary source of information on this offering was provided by the company itself, whose pitch was focused on the logical side of the brain that rationalises purchasing decisions. 'Nobody gets fired for buying IBM' is a phrase that anyone working in technology has come across. This slogan personifies the logical purchasing mindset: stay safe, go with the market leader and nothing bad will happen. However, with the Internet providing a massive new marketplace, and there being more competition than ever before, there has been a seismic shift in the way we buy products or services.

It is now thought that 70 per cent of the buying decisions take place before the company they are buying from knows the potential purchaser exists – this is the first shift. We do our own research online or via friends and come up with our own shortlist of potential companies to engage with. We no longer rely on marketing or adverts to make our decisions. We now place far more importance on the emotional reaction of other purchasers and less on the factual marketing 'blurb' from the company.

The second, more impactful element is that we now tend to purchase only from brands that resonate with us. By resonate, I mean share our values, match our view of the world, or make us feel like the person we aspire to be. The initial decision to purchase or not purchase comes from the emotional part of our brain – the limbic system. It is only after the emotional decision has been made that the larger part of our brain, the prefrontal cortex, the rational part, puts forward logical arguments and reasons to support the decision. The commitment to the product/service sits more firmly in the left hand (emotive) side of the brain.

These shifts have major repercussions for companies, as they must consider how to make their product/service resonate emotionally, rather than being merely the 'best value' offering. We often will purchase something because of the story it represents. We want to associate ourselves and support companies that have a heart, that follow a cause, are on a journey, or that have an audacious mission, rather than a more faceless and generic alternative. This may be irrespective of the extra investment we would need to make.

Brands need to have a personality, they need to stand for something, and they need to create an emotional reaction in the market in which they operate. This is partly why there's so much video content now being created. Sure, it's also down to our busy lives and having shorter attention spans, but fundamentally it is driven by the desire to make an emotional connection, which is easier by video than working through written copy. Make the emotional connection and the logical one will follow.

Essential elements & desirable attributes

To create an enhanced reputation in the eyes of both your existing and potential customers, there are three elements that need to be aligned across your business. Each of these elements answers one of the fundamental questions customers ask themselves (either consciously or subconsciously) when considering whether to spend money with your company. So if you can address these questions in a way that is both authentic and scalable, the probability of maximising your customers spend is significantly increased.

Maximising your existing reputation, as we have discussed, has a high degree of commercial logic attached to it, but it is difficult to do. It requires you to be honest about your current brand, and to do this with detachment and objectivity. It's not about how you see your company; it's about the view of your various stakeholders. This is not a quick fix, as reputations are built over years and months, not days and weeks. You need to be consistent over a period to build trust, admiration and your reputation. As Benjamin Franklin concluded, 'It takes many good deeds to build a good reputation, but only one bad one to lose it.'

1. Brand resonance
Are we telling our story well enough?

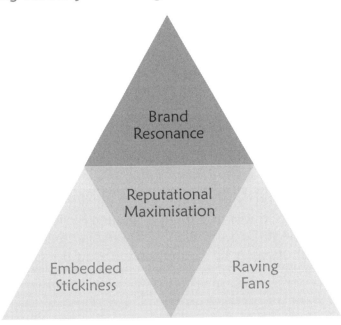

Not that long ago, producing something that potentially solved your customer's problem would have been enough to retain them. Now, unless you are operating in a very niche market, with few direct competitors, this is not enough. Beyond being a solution, your offering also needs to resonate with your customer; this comes down to whether your company or brand is desirable to do business with. Previously, the consumer had less choice – the power was with the seller or company. However, now there are numerous direct and indirect solutions that can offer a similar potential outcome, the power is with the consumer. This is why *brand resonance* is now so critical.

Our preference is to enter into relationships with people that we have something in common with; the connection may be a belief, a passion, a hobby, etc. The type of connection is irrelevant – what is important to establish a relationship is some element of commonality. Resonance is partly about sharing a feeling of emotion and partly about being understood. Brands that resonate with us are the ones that create positive emotions, where we feel understood, and our needs and our values are met. We, the consumers, have so many choices available to us that offer similar solutions to our problems that it isn't easy to differentiate between the offerings on merely a logical level. This is why our decisions become emotional; our feelings become the differentiator.

What this means from a company perspective is that their promotion strategy must communicate how their product/solution will make the purchaser feel. It's no longer about simply solving issues. You must resonate louder.

A good story has three key attributes:

i. purpose focused

ii. they are the heroes

iii. infotainment expected.

i. Purpose focused
What do you stand for?

In my job, I find myself sitting in on interviews to give my clients another perspective on the potential hire or strategic partner they are considering. One of the trends I am witnessing is a significant increase in the amount of time spent asking and talking about the purpose (or mission) of the company. More and more people are comfortable going to this level of questioning first, and increasingly use the answers to decide whether to work with a company. In the developed world, we generally have enough material possessions and monetary wealth to satisfy our basic needs, so our focus switches from our needs to making value-based decisions.

I think this logic applies equally well to all stakeholder relationships. Stakeholders want a return on their investment, whether the investment is monetary or time based, but increasingly they want to have an emotional return as well. They want to feel connected to something with meaning, and this is where purpose comes in. Simply stated, if your mission is just about generating money for shareholders, why would I choose to have a relationship with your company unless the 'offer' is too good to miss? Given that most companies don't have a competitive advantage that allows them to operate far outside the market norms (for the wages they pay or the price they charge), it comes down to having a differentiating factor that allows for a relationship to develop beyond a transactional one.

The great stories that are retold across generations are concerned with a mission or a quest. They have a degree of uncertainty around the outcome, as the mission being attempted is bigger, more challenging, or different from anything that has been attempted before. We have a high emotional connection with both the main characters and their journey; we want them to succeed. Ideally, a company is looking to generate the same connection and common desire for success with its customers.

➤ Why does your company exist?

➤ What big problem are you solving?

➤ What would be missing if your company did not exist?

These are the questions that your current and potential customers are interested in, these are the new differentiators. Like any good storyteller you need to set the context and explain the mission well enough to captivate your audience.

ii. They are the heroes
It is not about you

One of the many paradoxes that leaders must understand is the need to be a charismatic, inspirational leader, while simultaneously spotlighting attention on their people and customers. It's a hard balance to achieve, as part of the reason brands resonate is down to an inspiring personality to engage stakeholders. Particularly in the early stages of development, a lot of people may choose your company because of your passion. They buy the person as much as the company. If you are not front and centre, then a void can be created. However, as a company matures the clever leaders will make sure there is also another narrative being created. This narrative is concerned with the journey the leader, employees, customers and partners take together. Yes, the leader needs to set the vision and provide the inspiration, but they're not the hero. The heroes should be those on the journey with them.

If there are no followers, then there is no leader and no mission. Yes, JFK set the goal for a moon landing and provided the backing, but the heroes of that story were the scientists and engineers at NASA who made the goal a reality. Even the astronauts would acknowledge that they were entirely reliant on the engineers; they provided most towards achieving the goal.

For a company to attract a following it needs to be about real people and overcoming real obstacles. We want to hear from others who have gone before us, which is why we make so many buying decisions after hearing testimonials or trawling review sites. We need to hear from a relatable counterpart, not the head of marketing or the CEO, as their views don't carry the same credence for a potential purchaser.

Similarly, the culture of the company needs to be focused equally on the needs of the employees as well as organisational assumptions. Flexible working, remote working, job shares and employee reward schemes are all elements of this shift. A culture where the employees are acknowledged as the heroes as opposed to a replaceable commodity. Enlightened leaders appreciate the power that their employees have in either enhancing or diminishing the company's reputation.

A company needs engaged stakeholders more than the stakeholders need them – this is why they should be the hero in the story we tell.

iii. Infotainment is expected
How engaging is your content?

Infotainment is one of my favourite portmanteaus, as it combines the two requirements of a world-class brand message. We don't want to wade through lots of terms and conditions or website copy, we want a brief, interesting overview. As we now consume so much content, we expect a degree of style, panache or uniqueness in how it is presented. Our desire is to be informed in an entertaining way.

If you merely inform your audience of why they should connect or stay connected, then you run the risk of either overloading them with data or being forgettable in a crowded marketplace. On the other hand, if all you do is entertain them, but have no call to action, you risk wasting your marketing investment chasing vanity metrics such as followers, website hits, etc.

Resonance comes back to the necessity of appealing to both the left and right half of the brain. The entertainment part of your message will trigger positive emotions in your target audience, creating something memorable. Your information will ideally contain enough logic to satisfy the needs of the deeper right brain thinking.

The good news is that it's never been easier or cheaper to create this type of content yourself. The entry points are much lower than ever before and the technology we possess gives us the required capability. Therefore your main considerations are what you want to be known for, what your driving brand message should be, and what content best suits your target audience. Each of these decisions is critical, as every target audience has different characteristics; it is crucial that you align with their expectations. The bar has been raised when it comes to content creation and delivery, so you have two choices: raise your game, or get left behind.

2. Raving fans
Have you empowered an external marketing department?

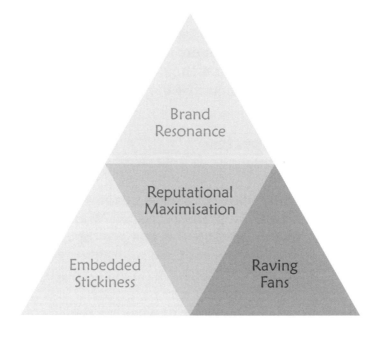

Once you have crafted a story that resonates, the next element you need to create a raving fan base to tell that story on your behalf.

Tony Robbins identifies connection as one of the six basic human needs that we search for every day. His theory is that these needs can be broken down into three conflicting pairs; he proposes that to be truly happy, each of these needs must be fulfilled regularly. Connection is paired with significance, as humans want to be part of something, while also being acknowledged and recognised. If Tony Robbins' theory is true then brands that give their stakeholders both a sense of connection and significance can fulfil two of six basic human needs. The simplest and most effective way to achieve this is to give them a story and a reason. Make them feel part of the brand story, rather than just being one of numerous consumers, employees or partners. They need to feel connected at a deeper level to your mission and have a significant role in the journey you're on.

Innocent drinks achieved a strong connection with their consumers from day one by letting them decide whether the company should exist at all. Their founders asked customers at a festival whether they should give up their day jobs to concentrate full time on making smoothies for a living. They built on this initial connection to grow their brand, which was later acquired by Coca-Cola in 2013 for megabucks.

Ben & Jerry's, the famous ice cream manufacturers, took this principle one step further, asking their customers to design new flavours for their ice creams. They run regular contests called 'Do the World a Flavour' and have a form on their website for consumer suggestions. Again, they created such a remarkable company that Unilever acquired them for a considerable return on their initial investment.

The 'Share a Coke with...' campaign run by Coca-Cola in the early 2010s, where they branded bottles with popular first names, was all about creating a more personal relationship with their consumers, inviting them to share their product with friends. They increased connectivity between the company and consumers but also between consumers themselves.

The by-product of increased connectivity with stakeholders is not only higher retention, but, as importantly, creating brand ambassadors who will be out there promoting your products. All you need to do is give them the story to tell and make them feel connected.

To increase the connection to a level where you have birthed *raving fans* there are three attributes which you need to focus on:

i.   retention comes first

ii. ratings fixation

iii. referral focus.

i. Retention comes first
Laying the foundations

It stands to reason that stakeholders need to be satisfied and ideally delighted before they recommend your business to others. This is why a high retention rate (or repeat purchase rate) is the bedrock from which *raving fans* can be built.

Retaining existing stakeholders should always be job number one. As we have previously discussed, there is strong financial logic behind this prioritisation, but there is also strong brand logic. Loyal and long-standing stakeholders are going to be more committed to the company and its mission; they perceive a relationship, rather than blandly transacting over goods or services. Before creating fans who care about the success of your brand, you must have sufficiently clearly defined and embedded ideal stakeholder experiences, as these underpin high retention rates. Make sure you understand how to consistently satisfy and ideally delight existing stakeholders.

For customers, this means creating a consistent ideal customer journey that can be relied upon to produce the required output time after time. This is about ensuring you have the right touchpoints (either automated or human) to ensure your customers feel valued, heard (if they need to communicate), and conclusively have their problems solved or needs satisfied.

For employees, this means creating personalised career paths and development opportunities, so their ambitions and needs are satisfied, to the extent they have no reason not to stay. It's about creating a culture where they are empowered and engaged.

For partners and suppliers, it's about honouring your contracts and then going beyond what was agreed. Meeting the basic agreement will satisfy, but this may not be enough to retain them. Going slightly beyond will create the delight, which will increase the probability of retaining their input.

Until you have consistent processes and systems in place to ensure high retention rates across all stakeholder groups, it's not really worth spending time and money on the next steps identified here. They will only work if you have established the strong foundations that high retention rates will give you.

ii. Ratings fixation

How much do they love you?

The second attribute of creating a base of *raving fans* is to understand who are the most likely stakeholders to convert into *raving fans*? This understanding gives you both insight and opportunity. It is far more effective to invest your marketing spend or training budgets on converting high-potential stakeholders (who are aligned with your ideal personas) into *raving fans*, than to invest a similar amount on all stakeholders. *Raving fans* will contribute more than the average stakeholder, stay longer and shout louder. Pareto's '80/20' law applies perfectly here, in that a small percentage of your stakeholders (20 per cent) will give you a significant proportion (80 per cent) of your positive reviews and referrals.

The first key action is to segment your stakeholders based on the quality and level of interaction with your brand, so you can identify the potential promoters within each group. Segmentation can be done very easily using widely available tools such as Net Promoter Score (NPS) or employee NPS software. Once you have clearly defined segments, you can then make more personalised messages and interactions appropriate to each group.

The 'promoter' segments will act as the megaphones for your activities, promotions and messaging if you give them the ammunition and collateral to do so. They will work in the same way as professional influencers, singing your praises to their followers. If these messages come from your customers, they will resonate more powerfully with potential customers, employees and partners. This is why your Net Promoter Score, Feefo rating or Tripadvisor star ratings are some of the most important metrics to your business.

iii. Referral focus

Are you galvanising your best sales force?

The final attribute, once you have identified the key segments, is to give your most ardent supporters a role in the future growth of your company. This might seem a little far fetched, but as I have previously suggested people want a connection with brands they feel passionate about – they revel in the power of this association. The main consideration is finding ways they can be part of the journey while satisfying both your and their needs.

Many companies will use their fans as part of their research and development, both in the design and testing of new offerings. This early feedback from the stakeholder segments most engaged with your mission can be very informative and save time and money. This testing gauges how new offerings are likely to resonate before you commit substantial investments into them. Beyond this, the most value these segments can offer is as brand ambassadors, your unofficial marketing and sales department. As previously identified, they have more creditability with your potential stakeholders and their opinions have higher value than your own marketing collateral.

Your fans are seen as independent thinkers who promote your company for no other reason than they love what you do. In reality, they may be receiving some direct or indirect benefit; this is true, but they still possess more widely trusted opinions. We choose to stay in hotels or book an Airbnb that other people rate highly, even though will never meet them and may have very different tastes. The fact they have taken the time to leave positive feedback is enough.

If you don't have referral schemes in place that encourage and reward your current customers, you are missing out on the highest quality leads you can generate. These leads already have a positive pre-engagement opinion based on what your current customers have told them. Referred customers are a salesperson's dream as they take a lot less 'warming-up' than fresh prospects.

You will already have *raving fans* in your business, so all you need to do is create the right environment, the right connection and the right incentives for them to become your brand ambassadors.

3. Embedded stickiness
Are we creating strong enough relationships?

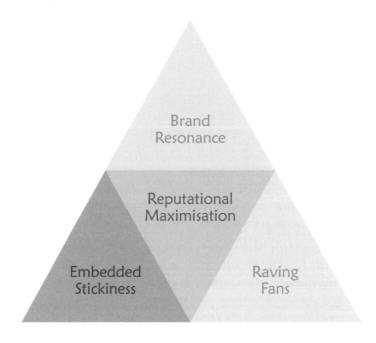

The final element that will maximise your reputation is to ensure there is the optimal amount of stickiness between you and your stakeholders. The concept of stickiness was originally a marketing term, used to describe how well a brand resonates with customers, but I think there is a business-wide relevance across all relationships.

Stickiness simply means the commitment or attachment to a person, a cause or a belief. Organisations that create a high degree of stickiness will not only have stakeholders that stay with them for longer, but these stakeholders will also be more committed with the way and frequency in which they interact with them.

Stickiness is important for a number of reasons. First, there is more competition than ever before, so without the required adherence to your brand, organisations will have to be continually churning relationships, always requiring new ones just to maintain their current level of output. Replacing stakeholders requires additional time and investment, which negatively impacts profitability. Second, stickiness across your various stakeholder groups will give you consistency and predictability from both a financial and resourcing perspective; this means you can operate your business more efficiently. Third, stickiness will generate a higher output from each stakeholder. The higher the attachment a stakeholder has to your purpose and leadership, the more you will get from them. Customers will spend more, employees will be more productive and suppliers will be more collaborative. Having strong and sticky foundational relationships across all stakeholder groups will help your business scale quicker and with greater confidence.

For the optimal degree of stickiness to be in place there are three attributes to focus on:

i.   consistently craved

ii. anticipating needs

iii. personalisation prioritised.

i. Consistent experience
Have we created the optimal stakeholder experiences?

Having repeatable processes and systems ingrained into the way the business operates will ensure that there is a consistency to stakeholder experiences. The goal is that each stakeholder is treated as a fundamental part of the company and gets a reliable service each time they interact with it. They need to feel that you care about them and the quality of experience they receive. By building processes and systems that optimise the impression you create, you are building the connection and adherence to each stakeholder. It's human nature to repeat pleasurable experiences that gave us the outcomes we hoped for.

When designing optimal experiences it is essential that you appreciate the position of your audience: what is the current situation like for one of your customers, employees or suppliers? We've all stayed in hotel rooms which are poorly designed, with light switches that don't work and sockets hidden in unhelpful corners. When this happens it is obvious that those who designed the experience haven't tested it first, which is why the experience is suboptimal.

Not enough adolescent companies invest sufficiently in systemisation to embed the ideal experiences they want to provide. They tend to leave too much leeway and don't have the necessary feedback and quality control systems in place to monitor the experience to the level required. This under-investment means they will struggle to maintain stakeholder experience as they scale the business; this leads to inconsistency and, therefore, reduced *stickiness*.

The reason companies like McDonald's are able to grow so quickly is predominantly down to the meticulously designed and rigorously enforced service delivery system: customers received exactly the same quality and speed of service whichever McDonald's they visited. In the same way, Amazon has grown exponentially over the past decade primarily because they have created an ultra-quick search, order and delivery mechanism. Consequently, they have become the default option for many people when looking to purchase online. Their consistency and predictability mean we don't bother comparing their offerings to others, we simply make two clicks and our order is on its way.

Consistency sounds easy to achieve but to embed and deliver it to all the different stakeholder groups simultaneously takes time and focus. The increased *stickiness* this will create makes it a prudent investment.

ii. Anticipating needs
You answer before they ask

Another bar that has been raised by the best companies is anticipating needs in advance. If you are able to offer me what I need before I even ask, my impression of you is going to be enhanced.

As consumers/purchasers we want to do business with companies who understand our needs. You will see so many more websites now boasting a very prominent FAQ (frequently asked questions) section. There are automated bots built into these sites to engage and direct us before we request assistance. There are webinars galore giving us information in advance of any purchase.

This principle is embedded in a number of service-based industries; a good example of one would be a five-star hotel, whose whole service ethos is built around anticipating and satisfying their guests' needs in advance of being asked to do so. The waiter working in the restaurant will ensure your wine glass is continually topped up, the front desk knows what newspaper you would like delivered with your breakfast in the morning, and the room maid will know exactly what type of coffee to have available during your stay. They achieve this level of excellence by a combination of obsession with customer preferences and cleverly constructed customer journeys; these capture past behaviours that allow them to anticipate future needs.

We all leave a lot of breadcrumbs these days around the Internet, our social media, and previous interactions which the savvy companies collect. They use this data to construct an experience that feels like it has been lovingly crafted just for us, although we know this cannot be true.

Just by answering the top ten FAQs from previous customers on your website, it stands to reason that you will answer some of the questions that potential customers will also have. This isn't rocket science, just a logical use of information you already have at your disposal. Similarly, creating ongoing dialogues with employees and suppliers about what it's like to work for/with you and what could improve the experience is a very low-cost activity. However, it can yield a disproportionally high return if you act on the feedback received. This information also allows you to iterate the experiences and interactions so that future employees and suppliers receive a better version of both.

We can find out a lot about potential customers, employees and suppliers in advance of any meetings or dialogues via a few quick online searches. Therefore there's no reason why we can't anticipate some of their needs ahead of their requests. This is easy to do and remarkably powerful if you get right.

iii. Personalisation prioritised
Are you making it just for me?

Consistency and anticipating needs will engender a high degree of connection if they are done in an authentic manner, but the attribute that has the greatest impact on *stickiness* is personalisation. Can you adapt your offering, so it fits like a glove, like it's been made just for me?

For some, offering personalisation is one of the core components and every item is made for a specific individual, such as a bespoke suit or wedding dress, so they have continued adherence and connection baked into their offering. For the rest of us it's a case of working out how far we can move down the generic/bespoke continuum and still remain profitable. At the generic end of the continuum there is no personalisation, and at the other is a completely unique offering. The generic product has the advantage of minimised production and delivery costs, but there is very little room to create a memorable experience, so the adhesion level of customers is very low. The more you move towards a bespoke solution, the more cost you build into production and/or delivery; however, you do improve the *stickiness* as there is greater differentiation and a more personalised experience is created. The key is finding the optimal balance point for your specific offering that makes you remarkable enough but still enables you to generate a worthwhile profit.

The pursuit of personalisation needs to apply to all stakeholder relationships if you wish to form an amazing reputation as an organisation. You will require people on the leadership team that have not only strong technical skills but creative minds, who can work away from the script and are comfortable finding the optimal solution in any given situation. This thinking aligns with one of the previous elements – *stakeholder reciprocation* – where I recommended that you made it about them and not just you.

Personalising experiences takes courage, creativity and commitment but the *stickiness* that can be generated is invaluable in the pursuit of a successful, growing business.

Case study
David Hieatt

David Hieatt is a true entrepreneur as well as being an expert in fashion, retail, sustainability and branding. He has created three distinctive and internationally acclaimed brands from scratch, Howies, Hiut Denim and Do Lectures. His early career was spent as a copywriter with Saatchi and Saatchi; this may explain the effective communication of his passion, and the commonality present in his vibrant brand. Hieatt instinctively knows how to build and grow a reputation that magnetically attracts followers.

Creating *brand resonance* has enabled all of his companies to punch above their weight. Hieatt's marketing philosophy is built on spending time crafting engaging copy rather than pouring valuable finances into marketing campaigns. Less is more when it comes to both copy and spends. The successes this strategy has continually produced across his ventures can partly be explained by keeping his driving purpose and philosophy front and centre. It may also be down to spotlighting his employees, collaborators and his customers, or maybe explained by the entertaining copy he creates, which challenges people's thinking.

Hieatt's brands resonate with the ideal audiences; all his companies are adept at making their customers the story. He has given them a number of outlets to broadcast positive feedback and incentives for them to do this, birthing *raving fans* not just passive consumers. He focuses on two things expertly: first, creating a high-quality product in a limited supply to increase demand, and second, thoroughly communicating the brand values and the reasons for doing things. Fans love the back story and now, more than ever, want to be associated with brands on a mission. Hieatt's companies cater to this desire excellently.

Once Hieatt created his community of fans, he developed a strong customer service arm and visible social media presence so his businesses could both respond to customer needs and, crucially, stay ahead of market expectations. These twin pillars generate the optimal embedded *stickiness* across their communities. There are cost offers to upgrade, upsell and refer others, but this strategy is implemented subtly through a combination of engaging copy and time-limited offers. Hieatt appreciated that manufacturing a limited number of high-quality offerings meant he could not only charge a premium price, but also create a demand curve that could outstrip the supply if desired.

All of Hieatt's companies are built around a relatively small core team but compensate by working with an extensive collection of collaborators and contributors. This strategy enables them to compete on a global stage (Do Lectures was voted one of the top ten idea festivals in the world) while keeping core costs low. Hieatt effectively cuts through the noise and competition by focusing on creating brands that have a clear and unique purpose that is cleverly articulated to maximising their reputation. He understands the power of communities with common shared purposes. Hieatt is undoubtedly an inspirational leader but is also a maverick maker who loves building brands that matter.

Key takeaways
Summary

Reputational maximisation and the mantra of *better before bigger*

In relation to the mantra *bigger before better* it's all about being conscious of both the impact you wish to create and which market(s) you want to create it in. Adolescent stage companies can become too obsessed with serving the maximum amount of people in sometimes very different markets. They are guilty of trying to be all things to all people, which only mega-brands such as Google and Amazon can actually do. Being *better before bigger* is about identifying which stakeholders and market suit and do not suit your company. Engage in ideal relationships.

Having the reputation for being the best in your sector is very different from being the biggest. The former is much easier to defend as a position as you are in control of more of the factors. It also means you are focused correctly on prioritising profit and sustainability over turnover and other vanity metrics.

Reputational maximisation and the paradox of *flucture*

To maximise your reputation you need to have in place a clear set of processes surrounding the way you interact with stakeholders and your method of operating your business. In adolescence, businesses can often turn out predictable experiences to stakeholders. Employees are measured by the company standards and aligned with the mission and values. This structure is a good foundation for reliability.

To counterbalance this increased structure, the ideal scenario is to empower employees to play the situation when appropriate rather than simply following the script. Yes, they need to know the script and follow it, but they can also be empowered to personalise the experience when necessary. This will create customer delight where possible rather than just satisfaction. Delight enhances a reputation where satisfaction merely maintains one. Structure builds the consistency needed; flexibility adds the differentiation required.

Reputational maximisation **and the concept of** *embracing the plateau*

What do you want to be famous for? Taking time away from the day-to-day operations and creating dedicated thinking time is key to *embracing the plateau*. You need to give yourself enough space to be detached from the brand to consider whether you need to change evolve or not. Do you need to reinvent, do you need to iterate, or do you need to amplify your current value proposition better? It may be that this would be a good time to work with a specialist brand agency to generate some different messaging and greater insights. What's important here is understanding why people buy from and work with you, which might be different from what you currently believe.

Once you have done the required thinking, consultation time needs to be allocated for articulating the revised brand proposition initially internally and, once clarified, externally. You must ensure your employees truly understand your brand position before you spend money and time repositioning (or amplifying your current positioning). This is about slowing down to think before accelerating to implement.

Reflect and commit

Before moving on to the next chapter, I would encourage you to reflect on whether you have a fervent and large enough fan base to sustain you through this next period of growth. What could you be doing to increase loyalty?

1 **Brand resonance** – when you look at the brand you have created, how well does it compare to other brands that resonate with you, which have their purpose front and centre?

2 **Raving fans** – are you currently focusing enough time and resources on your existing customers, or have you become too focused on new acquisitions?

3 **Embedded stickiness** – are you giving sufficient attention to improving the customer lifetime value and not just the number of customers?

Now based on those reflections, what are you prepared to commit to change?

I will start...
I will stop...
I will do more...
I will do less...

What's next?
Critical component #6: *Operational optimisation*

The final critical component is one that underpins all of the previous ones and that is *operational optimisation*. There needs to be an organisation-wide focus if you are going to achieve the ideal levels of efficiency and effectiveness in all processes and systems that operate throughout the company. For you to get maximum benefit from the other five components you need to ensure there is a culture of continual improvement to move you from beyond the status quo way of working.

9. Operational Optimisation

Organisational Fluidity

Operational Optimisation

Overload Avoidance

Continual Learning

Overview

Why is *operational optimisation* a core component?
Are you focusing enough on efficacy?

Efficacy is everything as you look to scale your business. If you are not operating near your optimal output then you are losing money, customers and time. Optimising the way you run the business is a key component because this will impact both how quickly, and how far, you can grow your business. When there was less competition and customer expectations were lower, suboptimal businesses could survive and even thrive if there was little competition in their chosen market. This is no longer the case. Competition is now everywhere, and the weaker businesses no longer survive. Their lack of efficiency means they have to work much harder and spend more money than their competitors just to be competitive; this position is unsustainable.

Creating an efficiently operating company which works without the direct input of its leadership should be the Holy Grail which all businesses aspire to achieve. The challenge is that improving efficiency is not as thrilling as generating new sales or converting new opportunities, so it doesn't necessarily get the attention it merits. Short-term thinking and an obsession with vanity metrics (like turnover) distract leaders from working on improving systems, processes and resource management which is the work needed to optimise operations.

How adolescent companies approach *operational optimisation*
The current challenge

During adolescence, the default mentality around systems and processes is to make do until the current way no longer works. I appreciate this is a sweeping generalisation, but far too often there's not enough joined-up thinking about what best practice looks like. The software used tends to be departmental specific, determined by the preferences of the person operating that department. Time is wasted trying to extract, format and disseminate information to other departments.

This inefficiency also impacts the way the work is organised with over-reactive approach, and not enough consideration to best organising workflows and people. Decisions that need to be taken are deferred to some non-specific future time when there will be more time/money to make the required improvements. Any headway that is made is generally down to an individual working to their own agenda, rather than through some grander company-wide plan.

How mature companies approach *operational optimisation*
The ideal scenario

To reach maturity, companies have to appreciate the importance and embed a mindset of championing system and process improvements. Even with an outstanding offering and an excellently motivated team, a company can't stay competitive unless it has eliminated obvious waste and implemented thorough processes in its operations. Adolescent businesses are too focused on working well within departments; mature businesses know that departments must function optimally together. Stand-alone, tailored software is replaced with bespoke integrated operating systems that enable data and understanding to flow seamlessly across the company. People are employed just to improve the systems and make the business work more efficiently. Systemisation, automation and optimisation are part of every leader's vocabulary. Everyone appreciates that their additional profit can be achieved by lowering operating costs, delivery costs and overheads. Best practices are routinely shared across the business, and time is spent looking externally for new solutions from various industries. Leaders should understand, measure and celebrate efficiency improvements as much as they value sales and new contracts.

Considerations

Optimisation can occasionally come from a massive shift to a whole new way of operating, or migration to a new tool such as a piece of software or platform. However, generally it comes from a series of smaller gains or improvements rather than a monumental shift. This method of optimising works in alignment with the principle of compounding; this concept normally applies to the way interest builds on financial investments. Impressive results can be achieved due to the consistency of reinvesting gains, so that future gains are layered on top of previous ones. This gives exponential growth over a period if you stay disciplined and keep reinvesting. In a business sense the same principles can be applied to the way you improve business operations.

Infrequently, there will be a need to make a single, big shift besides those occasions where it is about finding a better way to operate on a daily basis. There are seldom glaring holes in the way an adolescent business operates otherwise they wouldn't have reached their position, but there may be small inefficiencies either within specific processes or in the way different processes dovetail together.

The operational side of organisations has normally grown organically without too much thought having been given to optimisation. The speed of growth and 'if it ain't broke don't fix it' mentality are the main reasons why more time and money may not have been focused on improving efficiency.

To change this mindset and focus, there are three considerations to think about carefully.

Incrementalism
1% iterations are enough

Incrementalism is simply the concept of reviewing and improving on a continual basis. Creatives, such as chefs or artists, are known for being quite discontented with their projects; they are always looking for an extra ingredient to add, or a slight improvement to make. The Sky professional cycling team have dominated the scene for a number of years, and have incorporated this concept into their day-to-day operations. Their general manager, Dave Brailsford, introduced and embedded a philosophy of 'marginal gains', meaning every aspect of the team and rider's way of working and living was continually reviewed. They go into great detail (the pillows they sleep on, the weight of the skin suits they race in, calculating the specific number of calories that a rider will need to complete a specific race or stage) to ensure that they are always optimising. This is a great example of incrementalism in action.

Incrementalism requires commitment from the senior leadership team and research into other operational processes, providing a constant flow of ideas. This approach is also aligned with a number of proven business improvement philosophies. It is like the Japanese concept of *kaizen*, which translates as the elimination of waste. This approach also overlaps with the principles of 'lean manufacturing', which advocates creating minimal viable products for beta testing, then looking to improve subsequent versions. These principles were partly responsible for the dominance of Japanese car manufacturers in the late 1970s in the US and European markets.

For this approach to work successfully some of the elements prescribed in previous chapters, such as employee empowerment, operational dashboards and defined ideal stakeholder experiences, need to be in place first.

Scalability
Are we good enough to grow further?

As your business scales, there is always the temptation and natural desire to invest in a more complicated or sophisticated operational system. While this is sometimes appropriate, there is a contrary point of view that suggests the way you have become successful should not be lost or sacrificed. The constant theme of balancing structure and flexibility is once again vital. Yes, you almost definitely need to add better processes, but make sure they are tailored to your business culture and not out-of-the-box solutions. This is one of the many conundrums that leaders face when their business starts to grow. It needs a detached perspective and objective assessment to reach the best answer in each case.

While deciding when and how to upgrade your systems can be complex, it is probably easier than upgrading team members. It's quite probable that you have people on your team who have reached their potential. If you were to invest in training them further, they may not possess the capacity, mindset or even desire to move up to the next level. You have to show a high degree of both business acumen and emotional intelligence to make this judgement and, when necessary, to bring in a more experienced practitioner or someone with more growth potential. These decisions are tough as your team have probably been loyal and served you (and the business) thus far. You need to balance the future needs of the business with any loyalty you feel to a particular employee.

The duality needed here is a challenge, as you must simultaneously consider the present and the future. In my experience, leaders tend to hold on to current processes and employees too long. It is because of these tendencies that I recommend that you take a stance that is 20 per cent more ruthless and hard nosed than feels naturally comfortable.

Scalability needs to present in all areas of the business and as the leader it is your responsibility to make sure that each area of the business has the people, the processes and the capacity to cope with the growth you anticipate in future years.

Sellability
Are we creating something that others would value or purchase?

One of the questions you should be constantly asking yourself and your senior leadership team is whether you have created anything worth selling! If you have created something that has value to someone else, your business has become a commodity; if not, you have only created an occupation. As Michael E. Gerber, author of *The E-Myth*, observed, 'If your business depends on you, you don't own a business – you have a job. And it's the worst job in the world because you're working for a lunatic!'

For a business to be worth something to someone else there are a number of factors that come into play. The keys ones are:

➤ It must have built-in value in the way it operates.

➤ It must have contracted customers and/or ongoing revenue streams.

➤ It must have intellectual property around the products and/or services it offers.

And factors it shouldn't have are:

➤ too much reliance on the subjective skills and ability of one or more key individuals (including you the CEO)

➤ too much reliance on one-off transactions, or customers that are difficult to predict or monetise

➤ a very generic offering that can be easily copied or improved upon by competitors.

As I say, there are many other related factors that come into play, but by considering the three positive and negative factors, you should be able to make a broad-brush assessment of whether you are creating something of value or not. The strategy you have pursued to date may have been founded on short-term thinking and monetising opportunities, which is fine while you are gaining traction and presence within a market. However, to be an influential player, with a longer potential business shelf life, you may need to change your thinking and strategy, to create more residual value in the organisation. This is not essential, it is a consideration, as some people are happy to run a lifestyle business that generates them a good living without the desire to ever exit their business or sell it on.

If you are still looking to create a business that operates without you and that has a high residual value, then there are three elements that you should focus on to ensure you have optimised your operations.

Essential elements & desirable attributes

1. Organisational fluidity
Conscious organisational design required

As companies grow there is a danger that leaders can add more breadth and depth to their structure without due consideration, resulting in a very fixed and rigid organisation. This creates the classic triangle structure we often see in organisational charts, with one leader at the very top, a layer of managers/supervisors/team leaders next, followed by lots of employees at the base. Often this structure organically appears unless there is a conscious decision to implement something different. The 'perils' in this organically created structure are numerous for an ambitious, rapidly growing company. The main ones are as follows:

➤ Establishing too many middle layers, which don't always add the same amount of value (i.e. profit) as they cost. The classic 'middle management layer' is often identified as the reason for organisational inefficiency.

➤ 'Silos' are created across the structure with sometimes little interaction between the different departments. This can lead to an empire-building mentality – managers become very protective of their function and can get caught up by their own agenda, rather than implementing the wider company strategy.

➤ Large departments where numerous employees report to a single manager or leader. This will create overload and leaves too little one-to-one time to build effective relationships.

Unless addressed, these 'perils' can quickly turn an agile company into a slower, more cautious organisation.

The paradox (of flucture) in play here is that the ideal organisational structure for an adolescent stage business needs to be both fluid and structured simultaneously. Too much of either state will create inefficiencies and slow future growth.

Make sure the structure works for all stakeholders and doesn't just look neat on a chart. This is about creating optimal-sized business functions, not building departments, as was once the fashionable thinking. It is essential that employees simultaneously see themselves as members of the overall company, their specific business function, and where appropriate, project teams. Your job as the leader is to continually challenge the structure, so that your customers and your EBITDA are prioritised (see Chapter 7). We have all experienced the frustration of dealing with large businesses which have a multitude of decision-makers to work through who have not considered the ideal customer experience. This is the unintended consequence of ill-considered organisational design which has allowed the desire for structure to dominate the need for flexibility.

There are three desirable attributes I would recommend considering to avoid too rigid an organisational structure being established within your company:

1 accessible and visible leadership

2 project mentality

3 multiple leaders required.

i. Accessible and visible leadership
Your presence is not optional

One of the first things that can get lost in a larger, more layered organisational structure is the presence and availability of the senior leadership team. This can be particularly disorienting for long-standing team members who had previously had regular contact with them.

There is also a danger that leaders become disconnected from the 'organisational truth' and can make decisions based on someone else's version of events, rather than reality. They may end up leading exclusively from the reports they receive, without consulting with 'front line' staff. To optimise operations, they should use a mixture of both.

Employees want to see and hear from their leaders regularly, they don't just want a watered-down version of their vision, insights and thoughts delivered by a 'junior' manager. They may expect the opportunity to challenge what they are being told in a productive, respectful way. The leaders we respect most are the ones who are willing to address concerns directly, take on ideas and consider different points of view.

Leaders need to be visible, personally or virtually, at regular pre-agreed times. Leaders need to be accessible, so stakeholders can communicate directly with them when they need to. With technology both elements are more attainable, as long as there's the will at the top to operate in this way. This goes back to prioritising and operating by the guiding principles:

➤ **Be aligned** – demonstrate the behaviours you want to see across the organisation.

➤ **Be transparent** – tell them how we're doing, what's succeeding and what's not.

➤ **Be vulnerable** – be open to being questioned and challenged by those you lead.

ii. Project mentality
Ready, steady, go and then repeat

An equally important attribute to consider is the speed at which the business is operating internally. By speed, I mean how quickly ideas get translated into actions or policies, or how quickly a response to external changes can be delivered. One of the inherent downsides of having a larger company is that decisions can become slower, as there are more people who potentially need to sign them off. Delay can be incurred by further questions asked, or more evidence being requested.

One way to avoid this is to take a leaf from design studios that have a default project mentality built into the way they operate. By project mentality I mean setting up short-term, intelligent objectives and assigning specific teams per dialogue. Keep the agenda very specific, keep the timescale as short as possible, and the team consisting of only those who can directly impact the outcome. Where possible, recruit team members from across different departments so you address the 'silo' mentality head on.

For this way of working to be the default organisational style it needs sponsorship and gravitas from the top. An effective method is when a senior leader is the project sponsor setting the deliverables and timescales, but then taking a back seat during the project delivery period, only getting involved via progress check-ins. This way of operating has the added advantage of a leader being able to sponsor across multiple projects simultaneously. The big time investment for them is in setting up the project and reviewing the outcome, with low time commitment needed during the delivery phase.

As leader, one of your accountabilities is in identifying parts of the operation that are working below an optimal level, and then injecting momentum to make an immediate improvement. You don't need to be personally part of the project team unless you have a specific skill set that is needed for its delivery. By initiating the project and stepping back you are sending a message of trust and belief into the team to deliver the required outcome.

The more you do this, the better you will become at it, and the quicker it will become second nature. However, there is one more critical attribute, which needs to be in place for this project mentality to be implemented successfully, and that is willing leaders.

iii. Multiple leaders required
Natural leaders don't wait to be chosen

The most effective teams in a business, military or voluntary setting all benefit from having multiple people who can lead as and when required. Effective teams have a culture which enables and encourages individuals to take responsibility. These teams know that leadership works best when the most appropriate, rather than a single, designated leader, takes charge. As the senior leaders you are not going to be the most knowledgeable person in every meeting if you have quality people around you. This means sometimes it makes sense to take a back seat and let someone else take the lead for a specific project. If you condition the rest of your team to be followers, what happens when you can't be present in a meeting, on a project, etc?

Multiple leaders are a prerequisite for transforming your adolescent company which operates on a control-and-command mentality to a more mature version, which operates with an engage-and-empower mentality. Visibly empowering others to take a greater amount of accountability perhaps a little before they may feel ready is the kind of vulnerable action required here.

An organisation which has accountability spread through its structure by having multiple leaders at different levels has more agility and higher engagement levels than a traditional hierarchal company. Yes, there is a need to invest more in training and staff development, but the payoff is definitely worth it. Having multiple leaders gives your business more resilience, gives you greater capacity to take on work and prevents you (and your senior leadership team) being the bottleneck of productivity. A fluid organisational structure will assist you in optimising your operational output both now and, more critically, when you have matured. When this has been achieved, you will require the shared responsibility, as the stakes are higher and the inefficiencies more costly.

2. Continual learning
Why every day should be a school day

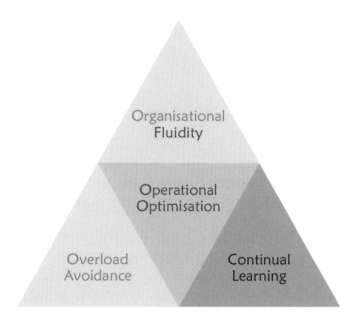

When you start out as a new business or as a first-time entrepreneur there is a steep learning curve which can't be avoided and should be embraced. There are lots of known unknowns (as well as a bunch of unknown unknowns) that you have to find the answers to, quickly. Resolving challenges, creating solutions and operating with little historical data to fall back on all become part of the day-to-day methodology you require to get the business off the ground and into profitability. Having a well-thought-out and costed business plan can reduce this learning on the job, but there is no getting away from the fact that every day is a school day to some extent. We are learning about our business, how to get the best from our team, and what our customers really want from us.

An enlightened leader/organisation accepts that this mentality serves their personal and organisational growth. A danger can be that we start to believe we've cracked it, and therefore there's no need to seek out new learning opportunities. In this situation an organisation can start to stagnate – not straight away, but gradually over time – if this behaviour is not challenged.

If, like an adolescent human, an adolescent company accepts that learning can be a lifelong pursuit, rather than a temporary period, then they can develop continually. It's no coincidence that most large profitable companies have their own research and development labs and/or in-house training centres. They know that they need to keep challenging the way they do things if they are going to maintain or improve their company performance.

So what are the key attributes that need to be present for this ethos to exist?

i.   personal development prioritised

ii. internal candidate bias

iii. no-blame philosophy.

i. Personal development prioritised
Are you giving your employees the incentive to grow?

I think the biggest barrier to learning within companies can be the beliefs and attitudes of the managers and leaders. If they have a limiting mindset and feel in any way threatened by their employees, then they may become the blockers, rather than the catalysts, for employee growth. Richard Branson suggested the approach should be 'Train people well enough so they can leave, treat them well enough so they don't want to.'

Leaders have a choice: they either make it personal, which means they will try and protect their position and status within the company, or make it about the employees, in which case they will support and champion personal development within their team.

As leaders we set employees' environment and expectations; we also have the opportunity to offer incentives and reward certain behaviours. If you operate the type of company that gives staff both the time and resources to learn new skills, you will be rewarded with a team of loyal, well-motivated and highly skilled employees. Alternatively, if you take a defensive, short-term approach, then it's likely that your employees will see you as a temporary workplace and will not give you their best or look for solutions.

It comes down to whether you see money spent on personal development as a cost or an investment. Going on holiday is a personal cost; going on a course to learn a new skill is a personal investment. Similarly, a forward-thinking, ambitious leader can see a training budget within a company as a necessary investment, whereas a more cautious leader would view the same budget as an optional cost.

Leaders should be looking to delegate as much as possible to those below them so they can work on new and more strategic projects. The only way this can occur is with an emphasis on training and personal development.

ii. Internal candidate bias
What's next for me?

Strangely, not enough successful companies favour internal candidates for jobs. The reasons for this are outlined below.

First, if there is not a training culture in place, it is less likely employees will gain the skills and confidence needed to realistically take a new or advanced role.

Second, unless their manager is happy for them to move onwards and upwards, it is unlikely that they will even put themselves forward, as they will think they are being potentially disloyal or disrespectful by doing so. They will need the support and endorsement of their manager to apply. In this situation they will need to know that their current role is safe and that their manager supports their ambition. Jumping without a safety net is not something most people will contemplate.

Third, they will need to operate in a team where employees push each other forward and assist their ambitions. If the team culture is negative, which either creates unhealthy competition between employees or doesn't value ambition, then it will be far harder for internal candidates to put themselves forward for new opportunities. Again, it comes down to the tone set by the department or overall leader.

The reasons leaders should engage and encourage their employees to aspire and apply are numerous. Here are some of the main ones:

➤ An existing employee by default must have the values you look for, otherwise they wouldn't have been recruited or still be employed by you. If you choose a new candidate you can never be 100 per cent sure that they will live by your values, however well they came across in the interview.

➤ It is both quicker and cheaper to promote internally than recruit externally. Current employees clearly buy into your mission and vision if they are putting themselves forward for a new role.

➤ You will gain extra commitment and loyalty from the current employee you promote, as you are sending them the message that they are valued, and you believe in their potential.

Obviously promoting an internal candidate is not always the best option and sometimes not an option at all, but by demonstrating you have a bias towards internal rather than external candidates, you promote the message of supporting your own. This will resonate across your workforce and other stakeholders.

iii. No-blame philosophy
It's not you, it's us!

The final attribute that needs to present is simply a no-blame philosophy. If your employees feel reassured that they will not be chastised for making an error outside their comfort zone, they will push themselves to develop further.

This can only happen if you have created a culture that rewards calculated risk-taking. If you, as their leader, suggest doubt in their ability or imply that they are being too optimistic about it, this mindset will negatively impact their behaviour.

I do appreciate in certain situations we need to eliminate risk rather than rewarding it, especially if there are serious consequences if things don't transpire as hoped. In most scenarios, there may be a slight reputational risk, maybe some financial risk or a lost opportunity risk, but all of these can be offset by the potential upside of the more autonomous, more creative workforce you stand to build. Vulnerability needs to be championed.

Organisational growth can only occur if there is initially personal growth among employees, and this growth is more likely to occur if a no-blame culture exists. The best teams succeed as one and fail as one; there is a collective responsibility in place.

If employees witness or hear of other employees being reprimanded for 'failure' in any form, this will naturally discourage them from putting themselves forward or suggesting anything new. This discouragement can be conscious or subconscious. In contrast, if they see that employees are actively thanked and recognised for their innovative thinking or can-do mentality, this will increase their own curiosity around what is possible for them.

As with the majority of the recommendations I put forward in this book, this isn't necessarily complicated. It's about understanding basic human behaviour and leaders developing their own emotional intelligence, so they are more tuned into the signals being sent from those they lead.

3. Overload avoidance
Why it's imperative to have guidelines

The final element of optimisation may seem obvious, but it is surprising how few companies have thought about the need for a communication strategy. When companies are small, the communication channels are straightforward, as everyone knows each other's names and are typically located in one location; there is regular contact throughout. However, as the number of employees increases as a business scales, this organic communication strategy becomes less efficient, as separate teams or silos start to form. It then becomes logistically difficult to have single all-company meetings and events.

Having appropriate tools, channels and strategies for both internal and external communication is required to ensure you have engagement with the core stakeholder groups. It is also one of the key drivers behind improving, or at least maintaining, the level of operational efficiency you achieved when you were smaller. The tools, channels and strategies refer to here are normally put into a set of guiding documents which form the operational manual, basically 'the way we do things here'.

For some leaders, putting together guidelines on best practice can be seen as unnecessary, either because it brings too much of a corporate feel to their organically created, unique company, or more commonly because they haven't properly understood the cost of not having them.

Without a strategic approach and accompanying set of organisational guidelines, the danger is that your performance and efficiency will start to be inhibited by a series of 'overloads'. To overcome these overloads there are three attributes to focus on embedding:

i.   proactive prioritisation

ii. demand management

iii. minimising updates.

i. Proactive prioritisation
Being guarded with your prize asset

A *diary overload* occurs when most of your schedule is pre-filled weeks in advance with operational meetings, leaving little time for any other type of work. Your own output, and that of your key employees, starts to be negatively impacted, as you spend too much time in meetings, working to other agendas, putting out fires and responding to requests, i.e. working reactively rather proactively.

This is another situation where leaders must get comfortable with duality. Simultaneously, they should allocate enough time to support the existing team focusing on the current challenges, while ring-fencing time for considering the future and evolving the business. Otherwise, if nothing changes, nothing changes.

Leadership time is arguably the most important resources your company has. I identified previously that the most successful companies are operating with proactive not reactive leaders; this is particularly important in relation to time management. It is very easy just to operate on autopilot, responding to demands from your team, your inbox and your direct reports. This means you are probably spending most of your time working on the urgent rather than the important, focusing on short-term issues rather medium-to-long-term challenges.

Once again, the key is to find a balance between being flexible enough in your time management to support and lead your team, but simultaneously have enough structure in your weekly routine so you can systematically cover all areas of your business. As the organisation scales, you will need to reduce the number of internal meetings you attend. You should be more concise when communicating with your direct team, so you can allocate more time to partner relationships, evaluating future opportunities, speaking with key customers, and other long-term, beneficial activities.

The implementation of this shift can be made easier and quicker by first nominating deputies that can be present in some of your meetings instead of you. This is a win/win scenario – they get the chance to develop as a leader and you gain more time back to focus on important projects. As long as you have a good reporting structure in place, you will not be missed. The second action you can take is chunking your diary into designated time spent on different activities with different stakeholder groups. A controlling calendar gives the required structured needed to work simultaneously in and on the business. Designating time in this way means disruption to important activities is far less likely. We all like to be needed, but if you are serious about creating the business you envisage spend time on, the essential rather than the urgent is a crucial adjustment to make. This change in leadership style needs to be clearly communicated to those impacted by the shift, as to why you are going to work differently and how they are going to be supported.

ii. Demand management
How to avoid becoming a bottleneck

A *task overload* is when you have too many responsibilities for the time available, however well you organise your diary.

This overload has a number of contributors, the most prominent is normally *inbox overload*. As your business grows, so does the number of employees and therefore so does the number of emails across the organisation. Strategies and tactics should be put in place to manage this outcome. The more proactive leaders may already have one of the increasingly popular tools for achieving the mythical 'inbox zero', but unless these tools are adopted company-wide, no real progress is likely to be made. A more macro shift is needed here, where email becomes part of a number of communication tools rather than the primary tool. There are now a host of tools that can be used, and it is essential that before a business grow, a well-thought-through communication guideline is embedded. This is a situation where radical transformation rather than incremental tinkering is strongly recommended.

An associated contributor to time overload is *request overload*. As more departments and employees are added to your growing company, each department will need information or outputs from others. This will result in an exponential increase unless this is addressed. The key to managing this is to make sure there is a central repository for all information and documents that employees will need. These documents should never be left on individuals hard drives or stay within a department. The more documents that are made available to all (with relevant access levels in place where necessary) the fewer requests will need to be made. Once a well-organised and maintained central data storage facility is in place, efficiency will increase as employees will be able to retrieve information when needed, rather than relying on someone to respond and share information. This increased transparency and accessibility may be a cultural shift that will take time to embed, but the increased output it will generate makes that investment worthwhile.

Acknowledging and gaining wide acceptance that systems and processes that were once optimal may no longer be so is vital to reducing *task overload*.

iii. Concise updates
What do you actually need to know?

The final type of overload, *report/reporting overload*, is probably the hardest to keep in check, because as your organisation has grown the number of people reporting to you, and therefore the number of reports, will naturally increase. Again, the key here is taking proactive steps to reduce this overload before it has a negative impact on your own productivity. It may be difficult to find the appropriate balance point, as part of your role as a leader is to spend time working with and developing a team around you. However, if this takes up too much of your schedule, as with the previous overloads, this reduces your available strategic time.

I don't think you can ever eliminate this overload, but you can manage it by putting in place three golden rules, which need to be applied to all leaders and managers across the business.

First, use the magic formula of *five plus or minus two* (5±2) when it comes to deciding how many people directly report to you. If you have more than seven you won't be able to invest the time they need, and if you have less than three, you're probably being underutilised. Once you have seven you should either promote someone to take on some of your reports, or if you already have another reporting partner, hand over some of the reports to them.

Next, introduce *structured fortnightly one-to-ones* discussing role purpose, main deliverables and key performance indicators. These need to be complemented by a more traditional appraisal, probably with the human resources department involved. Importantly, these performance reviews should be just one to one; introduce more parties and you risk the quality of the conversation. These reviews should be asking just three questions:

1 What have they achieved?

2 Where are they struggling/being challenged?

3 What support/input do they need from you to overcome this?

The critical emphasis here is that they feed back on their performance and you are there to listen, support, and only challenge if necessary. This is you in mentor/coach mode rather than leader mode. Keep the agenda the same, keep the time slot the same, and build consistency into the relationship. If you can demonstrate what good accountability looks like to them and they then reproduce that with their direct report, you will introduce person by person a high accountability culture across the company.

Finally, insist on reports being no more than one side of A4. Make them as succinct as possible; you can always ask for more detail if you need it. Create a standard reporting template that can be duplicated across the company. This encourages those producing the report to prioritise and summarise what they know efficiently, training them to extract the relevant information. Brevity and clarity need to be championed. When it comes to reporting, less can definitely be more. Your time, and their time, is precious so don't waste it either creating or having to read unnecessary long reports.

Case study

Royal Marines Commandos

When I think of effective and efficient organisations, the Royal Marines Commandos (RMCs) automatically come to mind; being the best at what they do underpins both their reason for existing and their legacy. They are at the very top of their field and have achieved this through total commitment to excellence and a constant drive to improve every part of their operations.

For most organisations, inefficiencies and underperformances have financial consequences, such as redundancies or sackings, or even the business closing down. While these are high stakes, they don't compare to those in a military context, where mistakes can ultimately lead to loss of life. This justifies the need to continually optimise, review and improve everything the commandos do. Their lives depend on the quality of their planning, the effectiveness of its implementation, and their on-the-job decision-making. All these components are meticulously considered and iterated in a training environment before they are applied to a real-life situation. Scenario-planning and operational efficiency is ingrained; everyone who is selected buys into this from day one.

The first element of *operational optimisation* embedded into RMCs is the need for *organisational fluidity*. They operate around a non-negotiable set of values with an obvious leadership structure in place. However, they also appreciate that on a specific mission, multiple leaders may be needed to make various decisions simultaneously. They can essentially function as smaller teams with a high degree of transparency to consider multiple, sometimes conflicting, situations before the next course of action is determined. The crystal-clear objective and well-practised way of operating means there is a high degree of trust present without egotism; therefore detached, precise, decision-making is always present. Each RMC knows in advance what role to play, and importantly, what role others will be playing; this alignment breeds trust and success.

RCMs are continually pushed to improve by a combination of continual training and an organisational-level expectation. Simulation exercises are performed at the same intensity they may experience in the field to produce commandos that can handle pressure. This means that *active learning* is continually happening across the organisation, and every post-exercise or post-mission debrief adds to the organisational learning. This can happen effectively as a 'no-blame' culture exists, meaning any failure is viewed as much as an organisational failure as an individual one, encouraging honesty and cooperation.

The final element, *overload avoidance*, is non-negotiable. To succeed in any given situation it is paramount that unnecessary distractions are eliminated. Any information or instructions that aren't necessary to the completion of the mission are omitted, so individual RMCs are given the optimal opportunity to perform. Information is kept on a need-to-know basis where deeper discussions either take place in advance of the mission to clarify strategy, or in post-mission debriefs to identify successes and possible improvements. Information and updates are minimised on the mission to ensure optimal focus on practicalities.

The level of efficiency and clarity exhibited by the RMCs is probably at a level unattainable for most organisations but this doesn't mean they shouldn't aspire to it. The commandos always strive to be the best – this is an admirable target to aim for.

Key takeaways
Summary

Organisational optimisation **and the mantra of** *better before bigger*

While the concept of getting *better before bigger* can be applied in all areas of your company, one of the greatest impacts it can have is in operations. It is imperative that as you scale, you do so in a lean way, continually eliminating unnecessary processes and upgrading the way you operate. Unless you have a fit-for-purpose operational hub at the centre of your company, then any gains in turnover may not be translated to net profit, as they will disappear into operational costs. The crux of this continual drive for improvement is the degree of buy-in you have from your employees. If you can get everyone to understand the importance of this, and how they can make an impact, then having an optimised operational hub can become a reality rather than a desire.

Better efficiency equals better profits, which should translate to increased dividends to shareholders and higher rewards for employees. Therefore everyone gains if this can be achieved.

Organisational optimisation **and the paradox of** *flucture*

Efficiency gains are made when we can repeatedly produce the same outcome from consistent inputs in a more structured way. The more efficient, the less waste created. The less waste, the better the return on assets (financial, human or intellectual). At the heart of this is discovering the optimum way to operate and then embedding this into the operational infrastructure, so everyone is following the same script. The more processes that can be automated without losing the required level of human interaction to keep the business personal, the better. There is a balance to be achieved here, but generally more structure and standardisation is required in organisation for any company to increase in both size and profitability.

Organisational optimisation and the concept of *embracing the plateau*

Give yourself the time and appropriate resources to consider if there are better ways to operate your business. Embracing the plateau means refusing to accept inadequate aspects of your organisation; consider investing in new processes, better software and improved hardware. Some of your profits should be allocated to the operational team to reinvest, so that you are continually reviewing what is possible. You may need to invest in external contracts to perform part of this review process, as they will have more objectivity. However, if you decide to make changes to your operational processes, you will need the approval of other senior leaders to commit to and embed these new measures.

Reflect and commit

Before moving on to the last chapter, I would encourage you to reflect on whether you have created an organisation that can comfortably mature to the next level, or whether you need to update your processes, systems and default culture before you scale up. What could you be doing to make the company leaner?

1 **Organisational fluidity** – when you look across your organisational chart, do you see sufficient numbers of people who currently lead, or have the potential to lead in the future?

2 **Continual learning** – are you doing enough to assist employee development, so they compete successfully for roles at the next level?

3 **Overload avoidance** – have you embedded standard reporting templates and meeting protocols to minimise reporting time?

Now based on those reflections, what are you prepared to commit to change?

I will start...
I will stop...
I will do more...
I will do less...

What's next?
Conscious action required

In the last chapter, the spotlight turns directly on you. Having progressed through the book, you now possess the information, and hopefully have begun to act upon it. In order to effectively transform your business and your relationship with it there is a range of specific actions I would encourage you to take.

10. Conscious Action

Overview

Your starting point is simply to take a conscious action in a determined and intentional way. In my experience, far too many leaders get their business to a certain size and then lose momentum to keep punching above their weight. It's all too easy to accept the status quo and maintain your current level of performance and status, all too easy to unconsciously just 'exist'. I challenge you to up your game, get hungry, get uncomfortable, and become conscious.

Leaders go first
If not you, then who?

As author George Couros once stated in his blog (georgecouros.ca), 'Leaders go first, and if they don't, they are not leading.' Like most profound statements it is simple to understand, but much harder to embed on a daily basis. The reason I think it is difficult is because we confuse leadership and management and don't always recognise the difference between the two. Effective management is all about doing something well, whereas effective leadership is about doing the right thing and at the right time. Management is inherently predictable; leadership focuses on the unpredictable and tries to make sense of it.

As you review your organisational structure, I'm sure you can point to senior members of your team who are effective managers but aren't leading. At the same time, you can probably identify managers lower down the organisational structures that have the potential to become leaders. For me, management is a role, and leadership is a mindset. You can appoint managers, but leaders generally choose themselves through their actions and the way they interact with others. Good managers are common; great leaders are rare.

The danger of doing nothing
If not now, then when?

The desire to pursue pleasure and escape pain are subconscious catalysts that shape the changes we make. In my experience the majority of business coaching focuses on removing pain as the main motivation. A coach works with the leader to assist them in removing frustrations or improving weak areas of the business. While this can work in the short term, the motivation and impetus are short lived. I have found that gaining pleasure (and the realisation of a vision) is far more a meaningful catalyst and gives a greater injection of momentum. So, the creation of a future state that will give pleasure to you and others would seem to be the optimal motivational stimulus, and more likely to create the required momentum.

The chances are that your life is satisfactory at present, your business is doing well, you make enough money, and there are no immediate threats. However, the likelihood is also that if you have picked up this book and reached this chapter, then being merely OK is not enough for you. You know you can achieve more and create the kind of business that leaves a legacy and has an impact far wider than its direct stakeholders.

Loosening the shackles
Time to disengage the autopilot

Modern life can feel very automated as the use of technology and devices increases. While this can have positive impacts in many ways, the danger is that we end up operating on autopilot for a large proportion of our lives. We let the satnav dictate the best route, we let our inbox decide what we spend our day doing, we let our direct reports influence our focus. It can all become very predictable. I strongly advocate that if this description resonates with you, then you make a choice to switch off the autopilot and start leading from the heart and towards your own destination. You get to choose your role and you get to choose your script. There is no point waiting for others to take the lead, as that is your responsibility alone, unless you specifically delegate that accountability.

A company mirrors its leader to a high degree, so any changes you make personally will model the transformations you want to see in others and across your business. This is a crossroads where you can choose to remain dissatisfied and keep on keeping-on, or seize the opportunity to implement change and seek an exciting, expansive future for your organisation and for yourself.

Considerations

Creating a legacy
How would you feel if you didn't reach your vision?

In the end we need to be proud of our contributions and our creations, of our legacy. You have the opportunity to create something that has a far wider impact than you could have as an individual, but if you keep your business dependent (adolescent), that impact will be limited. By maturing to being an autonomous company, you increase the potential of your legacy. Your role, if you choose to accept it, is to be the initiator and guardian of this transformation. Your endeavour, drive, and determination to this point have given you the luxury of choice. You have earned the right to decide what route your journey will take from here.

Your dharma
Are you living your purpose yet?

Buddhism operates around a number of central beliefs, one of which resonates very strongly with me – the concept of *dharma*. Spiritual thinker Deepak Chopra, states, 'There's at least one thing you can do better than anyone else on the entire planet.' Your goal is to discover this, so that your life and contribution have the maximum impact. Therefore focus on the things you excel in, your superpowers. Do not become disheartened by your weaknesses – these may be someone else's superpowers. Stop trying to be all things to all people and find a role for yourself and a way of running your company that is aligned with what you're naturally great at.

All in
You can't be partially pregnant!

For the concepts suggested in this book to be implemented, the most important element that needs to be present is the emotional buy-in from you, the business leader. Since the majority of businesses have been created around the beliefs, values and vision of the business owner/leader, the passion and commitment you put in that will determine the level of traction these will gain across the organisation. This will ultimately impact the amount of transformation that will take place. If people can see that you are committed, they will join the tribe.

This transformation can't be another fad or short-term fix, this needs to be a new way of operating for the foreseeable future. You need to allocate time and resources to the programme. This way you can systematically build the business that you envisage block by block, and simultaneously give yourself the freedom to be the leader you aspire to achieve, rather than the one you feel you ought to be. For me, transformation, like pregnancy, is a binary state – there are no degrees.

You have a choice to make. You can carry on as you are and get a similar financial and emotional return on investment to that you currently receive. Alternatively, you can specifically focus time and resources on areas of the business that are not working optimally and improve the organisation incrementally. Your other option is to transform your business into a mature version with multiple leaders, empowered employees, engaged stakeholders, aligned operating systems and a clearly defined purpose, by adopting the mindset and principles suggested in this book.

Generating momentum
Make some commitments to yourself and others

The ten commitments

If you were looking to transform your body you would begin with a few conscious actions, like joining a gym, hiring a personal trainer, stopping smoking, etc. The actions suggested in this book are no different. Start by making changes in the way you operate but keep ideologies and guiding principles front and centre as you do this. You will become clear on your purpose and may initially feel better working through some quick wins to give you the momentum needed.

These are some of the quick wins you could look to put in place straight away:

1. Commit to your deeper vision
Move your focus from profit to purpose

Finding your deeper 'why' is core to this transformation process that I recommend; it should be about more than the money alone. By now you will have realised that there is no direct correlation between profit and personal fulfilment unless you do something meaningful with it. Profit is of course a vital concern for all businesses but let your senior management team take the reins in this area; you will be left with more time to focus on the driving purpose of your company.

The principle of cause and effect operates in all areas of life; businesses are not immune to this law. If you operate your business from an ethical standpoint where you are a net contributor to society, and to your specific stakeholder relationships, you will likely receive a positive response back. Treat your stakeholders with respect and honesty and you will be rewarded in return. Remember, you need to go first; you need to give before you can receive.

2. Dance like no one is watching
Release the emotional shackles

I want to revisit the wise words of Mark Twain:

> You've gotta dance like there's nobody watching,
> Love like you'll never be hurt,
> Sing like there's nobody listening,
> And live like it's heaven on earth.

My interpretation of Twain's words is that you must be the true version of yourself, rather than trying to be the leader you feel you should be. Sure, try and improve, but don't try to be something you're not. Leaders aren't all the same, although they may have similar traits and attributes, so go with your gut instinct more often, and don't overanalyse. Just be you.

3. Champion proactivity over procrastination
Just do it!

The 'Just Do It' tagline is by any measure one of the most successful slogans of all time. At the time of launch, in 1998, Nike had 18 per cent of the US sports shoe market, and ten years later this had increased to 43 per cent. Its power is in its simplicity and positive message. In the same way, just one simple positive action can be enough to start a transformation process. Your status as leader is influential enough that any actions you take will start to have a wider impact. If you start arriving at meetings five minutes earlier, very soon that will become the company culture. Imagine the change that you want to make and then take the first step towards it. No procrastination, no second opinion needed, just do it, and see what happens next.

4. Make a big commitment
Write your own eulogy

There is a great exercise recommended by two of my favourite business gurus – Stephen Covey (*The 7 Habits of Highly Effective* People) and Michael Gerber (*The E-Myth Revisited*). It encourages you to start with the end in mind by writing your own eulogy. On first reading, this may sound a little strange, but unless you know what you want to achieve, how can you know what actions to take? You would not embark on a car journey without knowing the destination and having some idea of the route. This exercise makes you focus on the legacy you want to leave behind by planning the ultimate destination. If you commit to this exercise, it will provide you with clarity. If you're then bold enough to share your outcome with significant others, it increases the probability you will stick to it, creating accountability.

5. Get curious
Act like an inquisitive four-year-old

An easy activity is to spend a proportion of each day/week operating like an inquisitive four-year-old, asking why things are like they are. Why do we still use that machine for this process? Why are we churning so many customers? Why do we struggle to recruit good people? Sounds simple, but the key to this commitment is not just to ask the question once, but to keep digging until you get to the root cause. This process was championed by Toyota in the 1990s, and has been described as an 'iterative interrogative technique used to explore the cause-and-effect relationships underlying a particular problem' (see https://en.wikipedia.org/wiki/Five_whys). It is suggested you should ask 'why?' five times to reach the underlying cause. This cornerstone of their thought processes became a key differentiator and competitive advantage.

6. Become bolder
Take calculated risks

When I say, 'become bolder', what I really mean is 'regain the bravery you had when you started out'. For most entrepreneurs, the early years are their period of maximum risk-taking, probably because they feel they have less to lose and they don't spend too much time thinking through consequences. As we mature, various pressures and influences make us naturally more conservative; we think or, in most cases, overthink the consequences. Unfortunately, this behaviour is unlikely to lead to the change needed in a transformation programme, so I would encourage you to adopt a more gung-ho approach. If you are unsure about a decision or action you need to make, just ask yourself two questions: what's the worst that can happen and what is the likelihood of that happening? If you are comfortable with that potential scenario and satisfied with the odds, then you are free to act. It's not about reckless abandon, it's about taking a calculated risk by assessing the odds.

7. Listen to your inner voice
Create a time and space for R&R

Now when I say 'R&R', I do not mean 'rest and recuperation'. In this context I refer to assigning dedicated space for 'reflection and reconsideration'. I find the opportunity for R&R activities as regularly as possible. I start my day with meditation and yoga, focus on the day ahead and reflect on the previous day's achievements. In addition to this, I also use running to get my creative juices and problem-solving abilities flowing. This is a very personal element, and you need to find what works best for you. The commitment is just to give yourself time and space to allow your mind to process thoughts, ideas and possible actions, without any background noise or input from other people.

Our natural tendency can be to fill our diary with meetings, projects and other people's agendas, but very few leaders I have come across schedule time away from the office just to be still with their thoughts and ideas. This time is so crucial, and arguably becomes more crucial the larger your company grows.

8. Keep learning
Commit to self-betterment

There has never been a better time to be a scholar. There is so much information available to us at little-to-no cost that, if we choose, we can spend our lives learning. There's no reason, other than a lack of prioritisation and commitment, that we can't all engage in self-betterment programmes. We just need to choose the areas in which we want to grow. The best leaders have always done this naturally and appreciate that self-betterment is a way of life, rather than a period. If you don't feel you have the knowledge and/ or skills to be the person you aspire to be, then find a teacher, follow a guru or just read a book. Commit to the principle of self-betterment.

9. Get an accountability partner
Embed a sounding board into your team

Not seeing the wood for the trees is a challenge that most of us have to overcome when passionate about something. We see what we want to see most of the time, rather than what is actually there. We listen to our limiting beliefs and don't question the status quo enough. One simple way to overcome this is to have an accountability partner, someone on the outside looking in to provide objectivity. This could be a mentor, another business leader, a coach or a trusted friend. Having someone you can share concerns with, bounce ideas off and hold you accountable will make the transformation process easier and more likely to succeed. Verbalising your worries can be both a great tonic and the first step to remedying them. Committing your targets to someone else will also increase the likelihood that you will reach them.

10. Daily journaling
Monitoring your progress

As well as using an accountability partner, daily journaling is something else that I would strongly recommend. I benefit from spending time writing down my thoughts, fears and successes, reliving them as scribbles in my journal. This ritual ensures that I concentrate more clearly on what I have or haven't achieved, and spend a few minutes considering the reasons behind each. This introspective glance backwards facilitates a more productive path forward.

Summary

Ultimately, the choice is yours as to what type of business you want to create and what relationship you wish to have with it. For some people creating a 'lifestyle' business is the best option, as this fits best with the scale of their ambition and the context they work in. For others, it's about creating the best business they can, driven by desire and ambition. I wish you well on the next exciting stage of your business journey, and if you're in this second category, I hope the ideas I have articulated in this book will give you the confidence, clarity and conviction to achieve something wonderful. You can create something that not only brings you great joy and fulfilment, but also to your stakeholders. This is *your* opportunity.

Wayne Gretzky, arguably the greatest ice hockey player of all time, observed, 'I notice that I miss 100 per cent of the shots I never take.'

Go for it!

Acknowledgements

Most importantly I thank you for being curious and choosing to read this book; this makes the time I have invested into it worthwhile. Without you this would have been a pointless enterprise.

I appreciate my clients, both current and previous, for providing the inspiration, the motivation and the live test environment for me to trial some of the content contained within this book. Again, without you, I wouldn't have had the opportunity to hone my thinking and ideas before they were committed to the page.

Specifically, I acknowledge Jack my assistant. You may have only been on the journey for the latter part, but you have made a telling contribution to the final book, and the readers would like to thank you in advance for making the text more concise, more consistent and more considered than it would have been without your input.

Similarly, I would like to recognise my illustrators, Jason and Jack, whose skills have added visual impact and clarity to my words.

To Sue, Paul and Andrew, my core team at the Right Book Company, I truly grateful for your professionalism, attention to detail and accountability. You have ensured the creation of a far better book than I could have crafted on my own. Thank you also to Alex for your work on the manuscript in the early days.

I would like to recognise the valuable contributions of my Right Book Buddies who have been a constant source of support, and a great sounding board when required. Thank you, Kate, Nadine, Ceri, Richard, Mike, William, David, Darren and Jan for your generosity, grounding and guidance during this journey.

I am grateful also to the initial cohort of beta version readers, James, Mike, Caspar, Anthony and Jayne, for going in early and wading through some stodgy initial drafts. Additionally, I would like to show my appreciation to James for crafting a flattering foreword.

Finally, to Jude, for always being there and believing in me.

My inspirations

We all need inspirational people in our lives that raise the bar for us. These are some of mine:

➤ Seth Godin for prolific, thought-provoking output on a daily basis

➤ Donald Miller for demystifying storytelling

➤ Tim Denning for simplifying the art of writing

➤ David Hieatt for reframing brand building

➤ Leandro Herrero for your challenging views on leadership

➤ Grant Leboff for reminding me it is always about them

➤ Tony Robbins for inspiring me to do what I do.

I know none of these people personally but consume their content regularly, so they are part of my peripheral team, whether they know it or not.

Thank you for making me more curious.

My Magnificent Seven: Suggested further reading

➤ **Blue Ocean Strategy** – *W. Chan Kim & Renee Mauborgne*
Want to make competition less relevant? If so this is worth a read as the authors challenge you to focus on creating your own market rather than competing better in the existing ones.

➤ **Deep Work** – *Cal Newport*
A thought-provoking book that asks you to consider whether you are giving yourself the best opportunity to create the level and depth of original thinking and ideas that you are capable of.

➤ **Influence** – *Robert Cialdini*
The author puts forward that the key to persuading others of your point of view is down to six principles that underpin the psychological element of human behaviours.

➤ **The Seven Spiritual Laws** – *Deepak Chopra*
A book to cherish. Chopra offers a life-altering perspective on the attainment of success distilled down into seven simple but powerful principles that can be applied daily to the way people live and lead.

➤ **Lead the Field** – *Earl Nightingale*
A timeless classic. A set of simple exercises that will enable you to adopt a mindset that will enable you to operate at your full potential more of the time. Hundred of thousands of people have benefited from Nightingale's wisdom.

➤ **The Five Temptations of a CEO** – *Patrick Lencioni*
A powerful wake-up call for all leaders that puts forward a series of simple behaviours that if mastered can enable leaders to avoid the temptations outlined.

➤ **The E-Myth** – *Michael E Gerber*
The book every entrepreneur should read before they start out, which articulates the central principle of working *on* rather than *in* your business.